STUDY GUIDE TO ACCOMPANY
SULLIVAN • SHERMAN • HARRISON

A Short History of Western Civilization

Eighth Edition

Volume Two: since 1600

Joyce E. Salisbury

University of Wisconsin – Green Bay

McGraw-Hill, Inc.

New York   St. Louis   San Francisco   Auckland   Bogotá   Caracas   Lisbon
London   Madrid   Mexico City   Milan   Montreal   New Delhi
San Juan   Singapore   Sydney   Tokyo   Toronto

Study Guide to Accompany Sullivan-Sherman-Harrison:
A Short History of Western Civilization, Eighth Edition, Volume Two: since 1600

This book is printed on recycled, acid-free paper containing a minimum of 50% total recycled fiber with 10% postconsumer de-inked fiber.

1 2 3 4 5 6 7 8 9 0 DOC DOC 9 0 9 8 7 6 5 4

ISBN 0-07-026903-3

The editor was Sarah Touborg;
the production supervisor was Richard A. Ausburn.
R. R. Donnelley & Sons Company was printer and binder.

Cover credit: John O'Connor, "St. Pancras Hotel and Station from Pentonville Road," 1884, Museum of London.

CONTENTS

Part Five: Early Modern Times: The Seventeenth and Eighteenth Centuries

Part Six: Revolution, Industrialization, and Nationalism, 1776-1914

Part Seven: War and Global Interdependence, 1914-Present

Map Exercises

INTRODUCTION

Welcome to the study of Western civilization. Often students at the beginning of their college careers feel a little overwhelmed by the amount of material to learn, even when it is interesting. I have designed this study guide to help you get the most from this course. Be aware that it is written not to help you memorize, but to help you think about what you are learning; to make it part of your experience. (In the process, of course, you will remember more of the material by using this method.) Furthermore, this guide will help teach you the techniques you need to approach such courses in the future, whether they are history courses or other courses in the humanities or social sciences. Good study skills are the same in many courses. Please read this introduction carefully, because it will tell you how to make the most of this study guide. Now, here's how to approach your course in Western civilization:

Read the Textbook

I know your professor has already told you this, but I want to add a few words about it. First, keep up with the reading. Read the required sections before each lecture; don't wait until just before the exam to try to read it all at once. You just won't absorb the material that way (nor will you enjoy it). Second, read effectively. Here are some suggestions on how to do that.

1. Understand the overall subject of the chapter *before* you start reading it closely. Do this by reading and rephrasing in your own words the chapter title and all the subheadings within the chapter. Then look at a map to find the areas you will be reading about to locate the region spatially. Finally, for the first few chapters, read the Overview section in this Study Guide before you start reading the chapter. (After you've practiced this for a few chapters, don't read the Overview until after you've read the chapter. I'll explain why below).

2. Read the chapter slowly and highlight or underline the main points. I mean the *main* points. If you are highlighting one-third of the page or more, you are doing too much and it won't help you when you go back and study. Some people recommend that you outline the chapter. If you have the time, that is of course very helpful. Most students tell me they do not have time to outline every chapter. If this is the case with you, then work on your highlighting technique; that is the most efficient way to use your time and convert the book into a study tool.

3. As you finish each section of a chapter, stop, put the book down, and summarize it in your own words. Then summarize the whole chapter in your own words. Don't worry about getting all the details; those will come later; just answer the general question, "What is this chapter about?" This is a very important skill, and you will get better with practice. Use the Overview in this Guide to check your summary of the chapter. Did you get the main points? Do not try to match my words; just be sure you've gotten the main points. It is most important to put your summary into your own words (just as I did when I wrote the Overview). You will find as the semester proceeds, you will get good at being able to summarize what you have read. Take this skill with you to all your courses (as well as to your work career later). It is a valuable skill, and good use of the Overview in the Study Guide will help you develop it.

4. Now turn to the Study Guide.

Use the Study Guide

The Study Guide is designed to help you do several things: 1) think about and assimilate the material you read in the chapter; 2) review the details of the chapter; 3) prepare you to take a test on the material; 4) remind you that each chapter is part of a whole picture by reviewing what went before and pointing to what is coming up. Each chapter of the Guide is divided into several sections, each designed to improve a particular skill. Here is how to use each section and an explanation of what each is intended to accomplish.

OVERVIEW

The Overview provides a short summary of each chapter. For the first few chapters, read this first to start to let you know what the chapter is about. After that, you should be able to orient yourself into a chapter by reading the main headings of the text before you start to read. Then use the Overview to check your own summary of the chapter. It will help you learn how to summarize the main points of what you have read.

MAP EXERCISE

It is almost impossible to figure out what is going on in history without a sense of where it is going on. Each time the textbook reaches a point where there is a geographic change, the Study Guide will include a blank map with questions. The questions are designed not only to help you remember *where* something is, but also to stimulate you to think about the importance of the location and relationship among things. The map exercises are designed to help you prepare for exams even if your professor does not include a map section on any given exam, so do not skip it.

STUDY QUESTIONS

Each chapter contains a list of study questions. These ask you to review the material in the chapter, but also to think about the material in new ways. Be sure always to support your general, theoretical answers with specific details. Not only will this give you practice formulating a convincing argument, but it will help you review the details within the chapter. Students often ask me how they can remember many of the details that are presented in a text. The answer is to put the details in contexts. (It's easier to remember the trees if you understand the layout of the forest.) As you work on these questions, you will be creating new contexts that will enclose the details you want to remember.

While you work on these study questions, do not just refer to the text looking for the answers. Many questions require you to synthesize material in the text and bring your ideas to it. That is what a good essay question on a test will do, so this will give you practice in that skill.

Each numbered Study Question usually has two to three questions within it. Don't be intimidated by this; it really isn't more questions. Listing multiple questions is simply a way to make sure you cover all the issues that are implicit in the first question. Therefore, the second and/or third questions urge you to elaborate on the first question. Treat each numbered Study Question as one topic. Listing several subquestions in this way is also designed to help you when you prepare for essay questions. Often essay questions are phrased as only one question, yet they virtually never require one easy phrase as an answer. Compound questions like these will help you get used to answering complex essay questions, and more importantly, practice thinking about issues in a many-faceted way.

Many of the Study Questions ask you to compare or contrast events with similar contemporary occurrences. These questions are important for many reasons, one of which is that you will remember things better if they connect to your experiences. Therefore, do not neglect these questions even if you know that your professor will not ask such questions on an exam. They are important learning tools.

The best way to work on Study Questions is in a small group. Try to put together a study group with other students in the class. Meet often and answer these questions together. Other people's insights might help you, and there is no better way to learn something than by explaining it to someone else. Students also tell me that discussing (and arguing) over ideas in such study groups has been one of the most rewarding elements of their Western civilization courses. And it improves their grades, too.

IDENTIFICATION

I have included a list of main people and events here as a reminder that you should have included all these items in your answers to the map exercises and study questions. As you read over this list, ask yourself (or better yet, ask each other as you work in a group) who or what the item was; when and where it lived, flourished, or took place; and what significance it had for the period under review. In this way, you can review your knowledge of these things and people. However, the most important way to remember these is not to memorize some fact about them, but to use them in context. Did you leave any out when you were answering the Study Questions and Map Exercise? If so, where would they fit in?

CHRONOLOGY

I have put an asterisk (*) by some of the people and events in the identification list. List these in chronological order. You will find that some of the items in the list happened at the same time. As you list these items, put a circle around those that are contemporary. This will give you an opportunity to review the chronology of events, and remind you which happened at the same time. This exercise will also give you a different context to consider the identification terms. It will help you remember them as well as help make sure you know the sequence of the main events.

SAMPLE QUESTIONS

Each chapter offers a list of sample questions that might appear on an objective examination. If you are in a small class and will be having essay exams, your work on the Study Questions has given you review for that sort of exam. What if you are in a large class, and have multiple choice exams? Of course, the material you have worked on has given you the knowledge you need to answer questions on an objective exam. All you lack is technique. Many students believe that multiple choice exams are easier than other kinds because the answer is there. All they have to do is find it. However, the main difficulty with such exams is that students often get themselves confused by the array of choices. The wrong answers on tests are called "distractors" and they do distract you from finding the correct answer. It would be misleading for me to give you sample multiple choice questions, because it would only get you used to the kind of distractors *I* write, which would not necessarily be the same kind written by your professor. So, the best way to prepare for a multiple choice exam is to practice techniques that will keep you from being confused by the distractors. Here's how to take an objective exam: 1) Read the question (not the answers). 2) Formulate an answer in your mind. 3) Find the answer that comes closest to the one you formulated. 4) Don't change your mind unless you have a really compelling reason.

Since that is the best way to take an objective exam, these Sample Questions are written as if they were objective questions, but without the distractors. Formulate the best answer. If you don't know, look it up (I've provided the page number so you can find it easily). Remember, these are only a few questions, so your test will have many more. All this section is doing is giving you some practice with this kind of question. You will have learned the content you need for objective exams by working through the Map Exercise and the Study Questions.

REVIEW AND ANTICIPATION

Each chapter in this guide closes with a few questions that urge you to think beyond the chapter you have been working on. These questions will tie each chapter's material to things that have gone before. These questions will also ask you to guess what might be coming up based on what you know. It does not matter whether you are right or wrong. What this does is give you further context that will make the subsequent chapters more meaningful (and thus easier to remember). It also lets you review previous material a little so it always stays part of your learning.

That's all there is to it. If you use this Study Guide as I've described, you will have all the tools you need to be successful in this course. You will also have learned valuable techniques that you can take to other courses. And I hope this Guide will help you relax and enjoy the learning of history. Good luck and have fun.

Chapter 31
Society, Faith, and Culture in the Seventeenth and Eighteenth Centuries

OVERVIEW

The society and culture of the seventeenth and eighteenth centuries were dominated by the tastes and courts of absolute monarchs. Profoundly influential literature and art movements emerged under their patronage while social patterns were changing.

1. Society. This section describes the social and economic base of seventeenth- and eighteenth-century society. Population declines and growths provided the background for changes in the social structure that remained resistant to much social mobility. Most people continued to live on the land in small villages, although changes in agriculture and patterns of production began to change traditional rural ways of life. An "agricultural revolution" that improved existing products and developed new methods helped increase yields. To increase agricultural efficiency, old common fields were enclosed. Peasants increasingly supplemented their income by "cottage industry." Cities grew, bringing new opportunities for some and new poverty for others. Even the basic institution of society, the family, underwent changes during the eighteenth century, leading to family life that is more close to our own. Women were considered subordinate to men, and the roles of women varied depending upon their social class.

2. Faith: The Growth of Pietism. New religious sects grew that stressed faith and social activism through private charity. These influential movements were not revolutionary, but they emphasized working within the political status quo to effect social improvements. Therefore, they were able to make a significant impact on their societies.

3. Culture. The seventeenth and eighteenth centuries were marked by cultural advances in literature, painting, architecture and music. Most of these styles (baroque, classical, and rococo) reflected and perpetuated aristocratic tastes. However, in the Dutch Netherlands and England the increasingly wealthy middle class began to make their presence felt as patrons of the arts. The lower classes also had cultural outlets that were different from those that had developed in the courts of absolute rulers. They participated in festivals with music, dancing, feasts and generally rowdy celebrations. They enjoyed sports that brought communities together. The most popular were animal fights and soccer and cricket. The lines between the cultural tastes of the classes were beginning to blur, as classes mingled at sporting events and lower classes became more literate.

STUDY QUESTIONS

1. What were the population trends in the seventeenth and eighteenth centuries? What are the results of population growth on the lives of people? Do we see many of those same results today?

2. Describe the social structure of society. Include in your discussion of the various social classes 1) where they get their wealth and prestige, 2) what their function in society is, and 3) how easily they might change their status.

3. What social classes are shown in the paintings illustrated in the text? How are these classes portrayed? What stereotypes of the social classes are shown in the paintings?

4. What innovations were so important that their adoption introduced what has been called an "agricultural revolution"?

5. What were the advantages of urban life? What were the disadvantages? Does modern urban life hold these same advantages and disadvantages?

6. Describe the significant changes that occurred in family life during the second half of the eighteenth century. In which class were women most likely to work outside the home? Doing what? Which of these characteristics of family life do you find the most different from modern times?

7. What were the characteristics of eighteenth-century literature? How were these characteristics consistent with the values of absolute monarchs? Give some examples of authors and/or texts to demonstrate your point.

8. In the seventeenth and eighteenth centuries, there were three main styles of visual arts. What were they? What were the main characteristics of each? Give some examples of artists and/or works to demonstrate your point.

9. How did the music of the period also reflect many of these same characteristics? Who were the famous musical composers?

IDENTIFICATION

TRY TO USE EACH OF THESE TERMS AT LEAST ONCE IN ANSWERING THE STUDY QUESTIONS

Poor Laws	Jonathan Swift	El Greco
Quakers	Henry Fielding	Rembrandt van Rijn
Voltaire	baroque	Versailles

rococo	Jethro Tull	G.F. Handel
J.S. Bach	George Fox	St. Peter's
W.A. Mozart	Molière	Gainsborough
Charles Townsend	Saint-Simon	Velásquez
enclosures	John Milton	F.J. Haydn
pietism	*Paradise Lost*	classicism
John Wesley	Peter Paul Rubens	Christopher Wren
Blaise Pascal	Jan Vermeer	*Night Watch*
Rousseau		

SAMPLE QUESTIONS

1.   The aristocracy was the highest social class in the seventeenth and eighteenth centuries. While they were not always rich, from where did they get the money they had? (p. 407)

2.   What country is known for initiating most of the agricultural innovations that led to the agricultural revolution? (p. 408)

3.   Most cottage industry was engaged in producing what? (p. 408)

4.   How did the increasingly wealthy members of the middle class use their wealth to try to rise into the aristocracy? (p. 410)

5.   What careers were open to unmarried middle-class women of the seventeenth and eighteenth centuries? (p. 411)

6.   What were the characteristics of pietistic sects? (p. 412)

7.   Where did paintings and literature often reflect the tastes of the middle class? (p. 413)

8.   What were the major common denominators of the golden age of French literature? (p. 413)

9.   Who wrote the most popular French novel of the period, *Grand Cyrus*, under her brother's name to avoid discrimination? (p. 413)

10.   What literary form was developed in England in the eighteenth century that was aimed at and reflected the tastes of the middle class? (p. 414)

11.   What is the main thing that sets the painting of the Dutch Netherlands apart from that of other countries? (p. 416)

12.   What musical instruments developed rapidly in the seventeenth century? (p. 417)

13.   What kinds of music did Mozart compose? (p. 418)

REVIEW AND ANTICIPATION

1.   You can see the middle class beginning to get rich and participate in cultural activities. What do you think they are going to want to be involved in next? Will the aristocracy be able to hold onto its privileged position?

2.   Do you think the arts will continue to reflect aristocratic tastes? Why or why not?

Chapter 32
Royal Absolutism in Western
and Eastern Europe

OVERVIEW

In the seventeenth century, the rulers of some European states were able to exert absolute royal rule as a political system. These states grew strong and shaped the politics of Europe in the early modern period.

1.   Absolutism in Western Europe: France. The origins of absolute monarchy in France began in the sixteenth century with the careful policies of Henry IV that weakened the nobility and strengthened the monarchy. Henry helped the state prosper by encouraging new industries and granting religious toleration. These sensible policies were not continued after his death, so the economy of France was weakened. Yet, the strong monarchy did persist to be handed down to Louis XIV in whose extremely capable hands royal absolutism reached its height. Under Louis' reign, the idea of "divine right" monarchy was articulated that offered a theoretical base for absolute government. He moved his court to Versailles and kept the nobility under close control. As a divine right ruler, Louis persecuted religious minorities and engaged in aggressive wars to enhance his power. His expensive wars left a legacy that made his weaker successors unable to sustain the strength of royal power.

2.   Absolutism in Eastern Europe. During the seventeenth and eighteenth centuries three states in eastern Europe grew strong and developed absolute monarchies. The Hohenzollern dynasty in Prussia carefully built its power on the basis of a strong military and fiscal responsibility. It was successful enough to be able to extend its territories. The Hapsburg dynasty of Austria was also successful in centralizing its authority and extending its territory. Russia under the Romanovs built its absolutist government at the expense of its neighbors. In addition, the ruling elites further repressed the serfs until they were reduced to almost the status of slaves. These states of Prussia, Austria, and Russia soon dominated the east at the expense of their neighbors, especially Poland, Sweden and the Ottoman Empire.

MAP EXERCISE

1.   Highlight the state of Prussia. Where is Berlin? What is the most obvious weakness of this state? What area would be most threatened by its efforts to consolidate its territory?

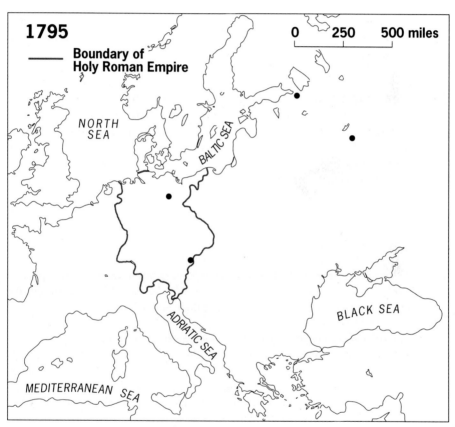

1795

—— **Boundary of Holy Roman Empire**

0   250   500 miles

NORTH SEA

BALTIC SEA

ADRIATIC SEA

BLACK SEA

MEDITERRANEAN SEA

MAP 32.3   Eastern Europe, Sixteenth – Eighteenth Centuries

See map on p. 143.

2.   Where is Austria? Where is Vienna? What states would most readily threaten Austria?

3.   Where is Moscow? Where is St. Petersburg? Why is the location of St. Petersburg consistent with Peter the Great's desire to bring Russia into closer contact with the West?

4.   Locate Poland, Sweden, and the Ottoman Empire. Why were these states vulnerable to their neighbors? Which neighbors took most advantage of them?

STUDY QUESTIONS

1.   What were the actions of Louis XIV's predecessors that allowed him to inherit a strong centralized state with a great deal of royal power? (Include both domestic and foreign activities in your discussion.) What caused the decline of French absolutism?

2.   What is the theory of divine right monarchy? What political philosopher was its main proponent, and under whose reign was it developed? In the reign of Louis XIV was this theory consistent with religious toleration?

3.   What policies did the Hohenzollerns of Prussia use to increase their power? What does the painting in Illustration 32.1 reveal about the things the Prussians emphasized in strengthening their power?

4.   What was the dynasty that ruled in Austria? What were the main policies of the ruler? What were its main problems?

5.   How did Russia grow to prominence until the Romanov rule in the seventeenth century? What did Peter I (the Great) do to increase his own power and the power of the Russian state?

6.   What social changes did Peter the Great introduce as part of his desire to model Russia after the western powers? What social group was affected the least by these changes?

7.   Did the revolt of Pugachev (under Catherine the Great) bring the status of peasants closer to that of western peasants?

8.   At the beginning of the eighteenth century, Poland included a large territory. In view of this, why wasn't Poland a strong state? (Include economic, political, and social reasons.)

IDENTIFICATION

TRY TO USE EACH OF THESE TERMS AT LEAST ONCE IN ANSWERING THE STUDY QUESTIONS AND MAP EXERCISES

*Henry IV	Huguenot	*Edict of Nantes
*Marie de Médicis	*Fronde*	*Richelieu
*Mazarin	Versailles	Colbert
Bossuet	Huguenot	mercantilism
Jansenist	Hohenzollern	*Great Elector
*Treaty of Utrecht	*Frederick	*Frederick II
*Frederick I	William I	*Ivan III
*Maria Theresa	Hapsburg	*Michael Romanov
*Ivan IV (Terrible)		

CHRONOLOGY

List in chronological order the words in the Identification section that have an asterisk (*). As you list these items, put a circle around those that are contemporary.

SAMPLE QUESTIONS

1.   What new industries did Henry IV encourage in France that helped increase the royal income? (p. 421)

2.   Which French ruler believed in religious toleration and increased prosperity for the lower classes? (p. 421)

3.   Describe the economic policy that has come to be called Colbertism and give its drawbacks. (p. 423)

4.   What was Louis XIV's religious policy, and how did it grow out of the concept of divine right monarchy? (pp. 423-424)

5.   What were the terms of the Treaty of Utrecht? (p. 425)

6.   What things undermined the power of the French monarchs after Louis XIV? (p. 425)

7.   What countries partitioned Poland in the eighteenth century? (p. 427)

8.   What Czar attempted to westernize Russia, and what steps did he take to do so? (pp. 428-429)

9.   What feature of the Polish legislature (the Diet) led to it being almost impossible to pass anything and thus to virtual political anarchy? (p. 430)

10.   In addition to Poland, what two other European states were weakened territorially by the growing strength of Austria, Prussia, and Russia? (p. 431)

11.   Why was Sweden unable to hold its far-flung territories, and which countries took its territories east and south of the Baltic? (p. 431)

REVIEW AND ANTICIPATION

1.   How is the baroque art described in the last chapter consistent with the political philosophy described here?

2.   What social group do you think was hindered by the economic policy of mercantilism? Do you expect a new economic theory to develop that will address their concerns?

3.   Given the increased oppression in the east under the absolute monarchs, what social group do you think will ultimately revolt?

Chapter 33
The Challenge to Absolutism:
England and the Dutch Netherlands

OVERVIEW

This chapter discusses the growth of representative democracy in England and the Dutch Netherlands during a time when absolutism was the dominant political thought elsewhere.

1. Early Stuart Attempts at Absolutism. James I and Charles I attempted to exert absolute authority in England. Their early efforts were frustrated by Parliament. Charles finally thought there were enough divisions within Parliament for him to try by force to become an absolute rather than a limited monarch.

2. Civil War, Commonwealth, and Protectorate, 1642-1660. In 1642 a civil war began between the forces of Parliament and those of the monarchy. Under the leadership of Cromwell, the parliamentary forces won, and replaced the monarchy. Ultimately, Parliament declared a "Protectorate" in which Cromwell was virtually an absolute monarch. Cromwell established religious toleration for Protestants, attempted to subdue rebellious Irish and Scots, and promoted colonial interests. Cromwell's son was unable to continue to rule. Parliament reintroduced the monarchy and placed the son of Charles I on the throne.

3. The Restoration, 1660-1688. During the Restoration (the return of Stuart rule) the old struggles between monarchy and Parliament continued, revealing an ongoing power struggle over who held ultimate authority. The problems were compounded by the Stuarts' support for Catholicism. Circumstances came to a head in 1688 when Parliament invited William and Mary of Orange to take the throne. A "bloodless revolution" had occurred.

4. The Glorious Revolution and Its Consequences. The "Glorious Revolution" was the largely nonviolent establishment of the reign of William and Mary. This change in government marked the victory of Parliament over absolute monarchs and the establishment in Britain of a limited monarchy. As a consequence of this victory, Parliament began to take an increasing role in affairs of state, and the political forms that mark Britain's system took shape.

5. The United Netherlands. When the people of the Netherlands won their freedom from the absolute monarch Philip II, they established a nation with a republican form of government. This government offered many freedoms

(including religious toleration) for its citizens. In this environment, the Dutch became leaders in commerce, art, and science in the seventeenth century.

STUDY QUESTIONS

1. What were the circumstances in England that interfered with the Stuart kings' desire to impose absolute rule? Be sure to consider economic, social, organizational, and religious circumstances.

2. What were Parliament's main objections to James I? What were Parliament's objections to Charles I?

3. Describe the course of the English civil war. Include a discussion of the supporters of both sides, and their aims. Who won? What was the main factor that determined the winning side?

4. What two forms of government were tried in England after the civil war until 1660? Why did each fail?

5. Who was initially brought to the throne by the Restoration? What policies of the Protectorate were overturned by the king? What problems remained? How did the Restoration period end?

6. What was the "Glorious Revolution"? What limits on royal power did Parliament impose?

7. Describe the "cabinet system" that emerged in the eighteenth century. What circumstances made its development necessary?

8. What foreign policy did William of Orange introduce? In what regions were most of his involvements? Are there modern consequences to his policies?

9. Describe the form of government established in the Netherlands. Describe the Dutch leadership role in commerce. Do you think there is a relationship between the politics and economics in this case? Do we associate democracy with free enterprise today?

10. Discuss the accomplishments of the Dutch in the arts and philosophy, and science. Do you think these accomplishments are a result of their economic successes or their political system?

IDENTIFICATION

TRY TO USE EACH OF THESE TERMS AT LEAST ONCE IN ANSWERING THE STUDY QUESTIONS

*James I	*Charles I	Petition of Rights
Star Chamber	*Short Parliament	*Long Parliament
*Oliver Cromwell	Cavalier	Roundheads
*Rump Parliament	*Commonwealth	Levellers
*Restoration	*Charles II	*Protectorate
Tories	Whigs	*James II
*William of Orange	*Glorious Revolution	John Locke
Jan Vermeer	*George I	*George II
Rembrandt van Rijn		

CHRONOLOGY

List in chronological order the words in the Identification section that have an asterisk (*). As you list these items, put a circle around those that are contemporary.

SAMPLE QUESTIONS

1.   The House of Commons in England theoretically represented the entire populace, but what groups actually dominated it? (p. 434)

2.   What caused the Scots to rebel in 1639 and invade northern England? (p. 435)

3.   What social and political programs did the Levellers advocate? (p. 436)

4.   Under Cromwell's influence, what position did the Rump Parliament take on the Anglican church, the House of Lords and the monarchy? (p. 437)

5.   What happened to Charles I after the civil war? (p. 437)

6.   Who was declared the Lord Protector for life of England? (p. 437)

7.   The Clarendon Code reestablished the Anglican church, but what groups were left out of the religious toleration? (p. 438)

8.   What bill passed in 1689 granted, among other things, freedom of speech to Parliament members and no taxation without representation? (p. 439)

9.   Who wrote the *Two Treatises on Civil Government* that established the political principle of government as a contract? (p. 439)

10.   What is the title of the official who leads the British cabinet and who is the leader of the majority party in the House of Commons? (p. 441)

11.   What treaty established the independence of the United Netherlands? (p. 441)

12.   In what industries did the Dutch grow wealthy and serve all of Europe? (p. 442)

13.   What inventions did the Dutch discover that played an important role in advancing the Scientific Revolution? (p. 442)

REVIEW AND ANTICIPATION

1.   Think about the policies of the absolute monarchs like Louis XIV of France. Were the policies of the early Stuart monarchs consistent with what they observed elsewhere in Europe?

2.   Review the religious beliefs and political policies of Philip II. How do you think his policies affected the form of government that was established in the Netherlands?

3.   Which of these countries, Great Britain or the Netherlands, do you think will be able to continue its leadership role? Why?

Chapter 34
Overseas Colonization
and the Competition for Empire

OVERVIEW

After the initial explorations of the Spanish and the Portuguese, many other European countries got involved in the struggle for trade and colonies all over the world. European culture left a profound impact on peoples in the New World as well as in Africa and the Far East.

1. The New World: The English, the French, and the Dutch. Since Spain and Portugal had established their dominance early in South America, England, France and the Netherlands focused their colonizing efforts on North America and the Caribbean. The English were the most successful, and were able to seize the Dutch and French colonies in the seventeenth and eighteenth centuries.

2. European Penetration of the Far East and Africa. The English, French, and Dutch actively established trading colonies to profit from the valuable trade with the East. The colonies in India and Africa were primarily trading not settlement colonies. The lucrative slave trade affected Africa far inland from the coastal trading colonies.

3. The Impact of European Expansion: Native Americans. When the Europeans arrived in the New World, they came with the expectation of making a profit from the plantation system or settling lands. Both motives caused severe disruptions in and exploitation of the native populations.

4. The Impact of European Expansion: The Far East. Europeans traveling to the Far East found highly developed civilizations resistant to European influence. India had a strong society ruled by Moslem Moguls with long-standing traditions and a strong caste system. Europeans established trading colonies on the coast to take advantage of trade. China, too, had a strong civilization ruled by the Manchu dynasty, and Japan under the shoguns felt so self-sufficient that they excluded Europeans from all access to Japan.

5. The Impact of European Expansion: Sub-Saharan Africa. Contact with Europeans disrupted much of sub-Saharan Africa, from the highly developed Moslem-influenced states to the native populations in the interior. Europeans looking for gold and especially slaves plundered Africa's human resources, contributing nothing in return.

6. <u>The Struggle for Overseas Empire.</u> The establishment of overseas empires caused European rivalries to take on a global scale. In addition, global economics and the politics of mercantilism further stimulated competition and struggle for empire. These motives led to a number of wars during the seventeenth and eighteenth centuries.

MAP EXERCISE

1. Locate the following: Russia, China, India, Philippines, Africa, South America, Mexico, Great Britain, Portugal, Spain, Ottoman Empire.

2. Mark the major colonies of each of the following European countries: Spain, Portugal, Great Britain, France, and Russia.

3. Look at the distances as shown by the mileage key. Which colonies were the closest to the European powers? Which were the farthest? How far was it from Russia to its North American colony?

4. How far was it from Spain to its colony in the Philippines? Why was it worth holding such a small colony so far from Europe?

STUDY QUESTIONS

1. What policies did the governments of Britain, France and the Netherlands pursue with regard to their colonies? How did the differing approaches allow England to become the most successful of these three colonizers?

2. In what regions did the Dutch and British establish trading colonies in the Far East and Africa? What role did trading companies play in the colonizing efforts? How much impact did the Europeans have in these areas? Why?

3. Describe the relationship between the European settlers and the native American populations. What were the differences between the way the Spanish and Portuguese, English and French settlers treated the native peoples? Which resulted in the worst consequences for the Indians?

4. Why was the European impact on the native populations in the Far East so much less than in the New World?

5. What system of governments did Europeans find in India, China, and Japan? What impact did the Europeans have on these governments?

0 1000 2000 miles

MAP 34.1 Overseas Possessions

6.   What was the European impact on sub-Saharan Africa? How was the impact different between the regions of Moslem influence and those of the interior?

7.   Describe the slave trade and how it influenced the political and social life of Africa. What states were wealthy before 1500, and which rose to prominence as a result of the slave trade?

8.   What economic policies contributed to the European struggle for overseas empires? What wars were fought over the domination of territories outside of Europe? What country emerged as the main victor of these struggles?

IDENTIFICATION

TRY TO USE EACH OF THESE TERMS AT LEAST ONCE IN ANSWERING THE STUDY QUESTIONS AND MAP EXERCISES

Cape of Good Hope	Mogul	Brahmin
Manchu	Asante	Ghana
Ngola	mercantilism	King William's War
War of Spanish	Queen Anne's War	King George's War
Succession	War of Austrian	French & Indian War
Seven Years' War	Succession	William Pitt
	Robert Clive	

SAMPLE QUESTIONS

1.   In what areas of the New World did the English, French, and Dutch focus their colonizing efforts? (pp. 446-447)

2.   What was the major economic activity in the French colonies of the West Indies? (p. 446)

3.   What commodities from the Indies did the Dutch successfully market to European countries? (p. 448)

4.   The Spanish and Portuguese viewed the Indians solely for what purpose? (p. 450)

5.   In what region of the New World did enough American Indian culture survive to give society a special hybrid character? (p. 450)

6.   What was the main reason that Europeans were unable to make much of an impact in the Far East during the seventeenth and eighteenth centuries? (p. 451)

7.   What was the dynasty that ruled China in the seventeenth century? (p. 451)

8.   A number of sub-saharan African states grew very prosperous prior to 1500. What brought these states their prosperity? (p. 452)

9.   What was the economic system of the southern African populations outside the sphere of Moslem influence? (p. 452)

10.   What did the Navigation Act of 1651 require? (p. 454)

11.   What economic system centers on maintaining a favorable balance of gold and silver coming into the economy? (p. 454)

12.   What did the Treaty of Paris accomplish? (p. 455)

REVIEW AND ANTICIPATION

1.   Review the areas of Spanish and Portuguese exploration. Where did this force England, France and the Netherlands to focus their attention? Which areas do you think turned out to be most profitable in the long run?

2.   Think about the chapter on absolute monarchies and the ways in which absolute monarchs worked to increase their power. Are the explorations and the economic policies described in this chapter consistent with those policies?

3.   Do you think Europeans will be content to stay largely excluded from trade with China and Japan? What will motivate them to push for more access to those countries?

4.   Which areas of the world do you think will have the most difficult time recovering from the effects of European colonization? Why?

Chapter 35
The Scientific Revolution

OVERVIEW

Beginning in the sixteenth century, there were new ideas and discoveries that profoundly changed the way people viewed the universe and themselves. These ideas transformed thought and society.

1. Causes and Spread. The causes of the Scientific Revolution extend back well before the sixteenth century. The ideas of the Renaissance and, less importantly, of the Reformation forwarded the search for new ideas. In addition, the printing press facilitated the spread of new concepts. Finally, seventeenth-century governments supported new discoveries as a way to increase their own power.

2. Astronomy and Physics: From Copernicus to Newton. A series of great thinkers from the sixteenth through the eighteenth centuries slowly built upon each other's discoveries to begin to understand the structure of the physical universe. They established that the sun was the center of the solar system, and studied the principles of motion that governed planetary movement. Finally, they could explain the universe by a series of mathematical laws.

3. Scientific Methodology. In addition to new discoveries, the new science featured new methodology that emphasized skepticism, experimentation, and reasoning based on observation and mathematics. Two of the main proponents of this new methodology were Francis Bacon and René Descartes.

4. Other Disciplines. The methods of the Scientific Revolution were applied to many other fields, including medicine, anatomy, chemistry, mathematics, and political theory, transforming those disciplines.

5. Impact. While the end of the seventeenth century saw the replacement of the medieval Aristotelian world view with the Copernican-Newtonian universe, the ideas and discoveries affected only a few people, and these were mostly men.

STUDY QUESTIONS

1. What was the view of the universe that had prevailed before the Scientific Revolution? What things facilitated the breakdown of that view and its replacement with a new scientific view?

2. Describe the series of discoveries in astronomy and physics from the sixteenth through the eighteenth centuries that led to the acceptance of a heliocentric universe that was governed by mathematical laws. Be sure to include the major figures involved in these discoveries.

3. Describe the scientific method. What skills does it advocate? What were the contributions of the main proponents of the new method? Do we still emphasize this method today?

4. How was the scientific method applied to the disciplines of anatomy and chemistry in the sixteenth and seventeenth centuries? What were the main discoveries (include both theory and technology)? Which of these discoveries has the most impact today?

5. What were the significant developments in mathematics? Why was the study of mathematics so central to the scientific enterprise?

6. What two political philosophers of the seventeenth century applied the scientific method to political theory? What were their main ideas? Which political theorist comes closest to our views of human nature and governance?

7. What was the impact of the Scientific Revolution on women in the seventeenth century? What women scientists were involved, and why weren't there more women represented? Are women still underrepresented today?

8. What was the impact of the Scientific Revolution on the masses of people?

IDENTIFICATION

TRY TO USE EACH OF THESE TERMS AT LEAST ONCE IN ANSWERING THE STUDY QUESTIONS

*Aristotle
*Tycho Brahe
heliocentric
Francis Bacon
William Harvey
logarithms
Leviathan

*Ptolemy
*Johann Kepler
*Galileo Galilei
René Descartes
Robert Boyle
William Leibnitz
Thomas Hobbes
Margaret
  Cavendish

*Nicolaus
  Copernicus
*Isaac Newton
Vesalius
Sir John Napier
Leeuwenhoek
John Locke
Sibylla Merian

CHRONOLOGY

List in chronological order the words in the Identification section that have an asterisk (*). As you list these items, put a circle around those that are contemporary.

SAMPLE QUESTIONS

1.   What were two scientific academies that were established by governments to advance scientific discoveries? (p. 459)

2.   What is the central idea of the view of the world known as the Copernican revolution? (p. 459)

3.   Which scientist had his views on the nature of the universe condemned by the Inquisition in 1633? (p. 461)

4.   Who wrote *Dialogue on the Two Chief Systems of the World* which popularized scientific discoveries? (p. 461)

5.   Who wrote *Principia* or *The Mathematical Principles of Natural Knowledge* which explained the laws of motion in the universe? (p. 461)

6.   Who discovered analytic geometry? (p. 462)

7.   What is "Cartesian dualism"? (p. 463)

8.   Who are regarded as the founders of the science of anatomy? (p. 463)

9.   Who laid the foundations for modern chemistry and discovered a law of gases? (p. 463)

10.   What is the language in which science is expressed? (p. 463)

11.   What political theorist justified absolutism in the name of law and order? (p. 464)

12.   What political theorist concluded that British constitutionalism was in accordance with natural law? (p. 464)

REVIEW AND ANTICIPATION

1.   Review the characteristics of Renaissance and humanist thought, and decide which ones would have been most important in forwarding scientific thought.

2. How do you think the scientific method and way of viewing the world will influence other aspects of society? Will it have an impact on social life, or economics, or other disciplines? How?

3. What do you think is the most important reason for people to adopt new scientific ideas?

Chapter 36
The Enlightenment

OVERVIEW

During the eighteenth century, a new way of thinking that had been influenced by the Scientific Revolution swept through European society, making an impact on all aspects of life and thought including everything from politics to economics to society.

1. Enlightenment Concepts. Enlightenment thinkers stressed three concepts in formulating their thought: 1) belief in the power of reason to solve problems in all fields; 2) belief that nature is rational, good, and governed by laws; and 3) belief in the value of change and progress. Enlightenment thinkers used these concepts to criticize institutions and customs of the past (including religious structures) in the hopes of bringing about a new era of freedom and reason.

2. The *Philosophes.* Proponents of Enlightenment thought were known in France as *philosophes* (the French word for "philosopher"). These people were usually not formally trained nor associated with universities, but were interested in the new scientific ideas as well as literary products of the age. Their broad tastes are reflected in the publication of the *Encyclopedia*, which summarized knowledge from their perspective. *Philosophes* were influenced by Isaac Newton, John Locke and other giants of the Scientific Revolution. The greatest French *philosophe* was Voltaire, although others, like Adam Smith and Jean-Jacques Rousseau, were equally influential.

3. Women and the Social Context. Women contributed to the growth of Enlightenment thought by serving as patrons of gatherings in the salons of Paris in which thinkers were brought together to exchange ideas. Women also contributed money to some *philosophes.* While Enlightenment thinkers generally supported improved education for women, they did not advocate equal rights for women.

4. Enlightenment and Religion. Enlightenment thinkers generally were in conflict with Christian churches in their view that an impersonal God was rational and had set the universe in motion, never to tamper with it again. As part of their rational approach, *philosophes* did advocate toleration of religious minorities (like Jews).

5. Political and Economic Aspects of the Enlightenment. Enlightenment thinkers turned their attention to discovering the most efficient and benevolent political and economic institutions. Influential political thinkers like Locke,

Montesquieu, and Rousseau wrote treatises that exerted profound influence on developing governments, and economists like Adam Smith developed *laissez faire* economic principles that continue to shape the modern world.

6. Enlightened Despotism. Instead of believing in revolution to bring about Enlightenment thought, many *philosophes* believed that enlightened despotism would be the best way to introduce reform. Several absolute rulers in Europe believed themselves to be shaped by enlightened thought and attempted to introduce such reforms. Since these rulers represented entrenched authority, most of their reforms were superficial.

7. Conclusion. The Enlightenment introduced a way of thinking into Europe that had a profound and lasting impact well into the modern times.

STUDY QUESTIONS

1. Describe the main ideas of the Enlightenment *philosophes* and tell how these ideas were expressed by the greatest Enlightenment figures. What did they attack, and what did they support?

2. What contribution did women make to the growth of French Enlightenment thought?

3. What was the Enlightenment's view of religion? Include in your discussion their position on the nature of God and on the treatment of religious minorities.

4. Who were the three greatest Enlightenment political thinkers, and what was the major contribution of each to political philosophy?

5. Who was the greatest Enlightenment economist, and what was his philosophy? What economic philosophy did the enlightened despot Frederick the Great adhere to? Was that consistent with his other Enlightenment policies? Why do you think he advocated that position?

6. Who were the enlightened despots, and what reforms did they attempt to introduce in their countries? How successful were they? Why?

IDENTIFICATION

TRY TO USE EACH OF THESE TERMS AT LEAST ONCE IN ANSWERING THE STUDY QUESTIONS

philosophes	Voltaire	D. Diderot

Adam Smith	J-J Rousseau	M. Wollstonecraft
deism	John Locke	Montesquieu
The Spirit of the Laws	*Social Contract*	*Wealth of Nations*
Two Treatises of Civil	Physiocrats	*laissez faire*
Government	Frederick the Great	Joseph II
	Catherine the Great	

SAMPLE QUESTIONS

1.   How did Enlightenment thinkers view human beings? (p. 467)

2.   What were the three most important concepts that characterized Enlightenment thought? (p. 467)

3.   Who was the great synthesizer of the Scientific Revolution who influenced the *philosophes*? (p. 468)

4.   What publication sold popularly and served to spread the ideas of the Enlightenment outside the major cities? (pp. 469-471)

5.   In the primary document, "The Philosophe," the author writes, "Reason is in the estimation of the Philosopher what grace is to the Christian." What does he mean by that? (p. 470)

6.   How did the ideas of Rousseau differ from those of most of the *philosophes*? (p. 471)

7.   In what way(s) did most of the *philosophes* support improving the rights of women? (p. 472)

8.   What was the major difference between *philosophes'* view of the role of God in the universe and that of Christian churches? (p. 472)

9.   What are the natural rights of human beings according to Locke? (p. 473)

10.   According to Locke, if a government interferes with an individual's private ownership of property, what rights and responsibilities does that individual have? (p. 473)

11.   Who was influential in developing the idea of a system of checks and balances in government? (p. 473)

12.   What is *laissez faire* economics? (pp. 473-474)

13.   What does "enlightened despotism" mean? (p. 474)

14.   What reforms did enlightened rulers attempt to introduce? (p. 474)

REVIEW AND ANTICIPATION

1.   How do the concepts of the Enlightenment resemble the ideas of the Scientific Revolution? How do these ideas contrast with those of the Renaissance and the Middle Ages?

2.   How do the religious ideas of the Enlightenment contrast with those of the Reformation? In thinking ahead to the American Revolution, which of these ideas will most influence the Founding Fathers?

3.   Which of the ideas of the Enlightenment political and economic thinkers do you think will have the most profound effect in the American and subsequent revolutions?

4.   What do you think will be the most effective way for societies to adopt enlightened ideas? (Revolution? Despotism? Some other way?)

5.   In the "Retrospect" section, the author summarizes the events from the Renaissance through the Enlightenment. Which of these events do you think were most important in shaping Enlightenment thought?

Chapter 37
The American Revolution

OVERVIEW

     The American Revolution was almost an inevitable consequence of the Age of Enlightenment and introduced an era of revolutions that was to dramatically change European society through the next century.

1.   <u>American Colonial Society.</u> The society that developed in America during the colonial period was different from that of Europe in many ways. In the colonies, there was a large population growth sustained by a varied agricultural base and a growing commercial trade based largely on export of raw materials. A new social hierarchy grew up in the colonies based on wealth rather than birth. At the bottom of this hierarchy were the slaves. Colonial society kept its European patriarchal structure, excluding women from most of public life. Religious diversity and freedom were more evident in the colonies than in Europe. The colonial system of government in which property owners took an active role encouraged colonists to believe they had the right to control their own political destiny.

2.   <u>The American Revolution: From Salutary Neglect to War.</u> Until 1763 (the end of the Seven Years' War), British authority largely neglected the colonies. Enforcing the mercantilist economic policy had a low priority. Afterwards, however, Great Britain began to try to enforce measures that were designed to increase revenues at the expense of the colonies. Americans reacted to these policies with defiant rhetoric and rebellion. When war broke out, colonial sentiment for independence grew, and culminated in the Declaration of Independence. After some colonial victories, other European powers supported the Americans, leading to a victory that bestowed independence in 1783.

3.   <u>The American Revolution and Social Change.</u> The American Revolution was built on the idea of republicanism which placed sovereignty with the people and led to a number of societal changes. This created a land with more equality and personal freedom than had ever been seen in Europe. These changes included establishing a political process with a great deal of popular control over government, religious tolerance, abolition of primogeniture, restriction (though not abolition) of slavery, and expanded educational opportunities. Furthermore, the war itself led to economic pressures that further equalized wealth and status among the colonials.

4. <u>Launching the New Nation.</u> Once independence had been won, the Americans faced the task of building a new nation. The constitution had to balance competing interests of a strong national government with power to the thirteen states. Two political parties developed, the Federalists and Republicans, that expressed differing views of how the government should be run. The electoral victory of Thomas Jefferson and the Republicans in 1800 demonstrated that a government could be created that would be responsive to the will of the people without having to resort to further revolution.

STUDY QUESTIONS

1. Describe the economic life of colonial society, including agricultural and commercial production. How did this economic life contribute to the specific social structure of the colonies (be sure to include all the social groups in your discussion)? How did this economic life help create a contrast between the social structure in America and in Europe?

2. Describe the religious life of colonial America. Which European churches grew up in the colonies, and how were they changed? What specifically American religious developments took place?

3. Describe the government of the colonies. How did this structure resemble the European past, and how was it distinctly American?

4. Describe the change of policy toward the colonies that led Americans to respond vigorously, and describe the nature of the response. Be sure to include the main figures and events in the Revolution, and include the differing political beliefs that shaped the two sides' positions.

5. What were the forces working against a close national union, and what was working in favor of one? Which impulse ultimately won out? (Be sure to notice the difference between the Articles of Confederation and the Constitution.)

6. What was the difference between the Federalists and the Republicans? Who were the main figures in those parties, and who won the election of 1800? Why was that election significant?

IDENTIFICATION

TRY TO USE EACH OF THESE TERMS AT LEAST ONCE IN ANSWERING
THE STUDY QUESTIONS

Great Awakening	Anglicanism	mercantilism
Pontiac	George Washington	Thomas Jefferson
Tories	John Adams	Benjamin Franklin
Treaty of Paris	republicanism	Bill of Rights
Federalists	Republicans	Articles of
A. Hamilton		Confederation

SAMPLE QUESTIONS

1.   What contributed to the greater population growth in the colonies versus in
        Europe? (p. 481)

2.   In 1776, approximately what percent of colonial population was African
        American? (p. 481)

3.   What were the chief forces that bestowed aristocratic status in Europe and
        in America? (p. 482)

4.   Who had the right to vote to elect the lower houses of the legislature in the
        colonies? (p. 487)

5.   What factors contributed to Britain's unsuccessful suppression of the
        rebellion? (p. 485)

6.   About 20 percent of the colonial population opposed the war. What happened
        to these people? (p. 485)

7.   What European country signed a formal alliance with America in 1778, thus
        contributing considerably to the successful war effort? (p. 486)

8.   What treaty ended the revolutionary war and required Britain to recognize
        American independence? (p. 486)

9.   In what authority did the framers of the American Constitution believe
        sovereignty rested? (p. 487)

10.   What European inheritance practice did the Americans abolish so that it
        would be easier for people to gain ownership of property? (p. 487)

11.   What effect did the Revolution have on slavery? (p. 487)

12.   What political party in the eighteenth century supported a strong national government? (pp. 488-489)

13.   Who won the election of 1800? (p. 490)

14.   Who presided over the Constitutional Convention in 1787? (Figure 37.1)

REVIEW AND ANTICIPATION

1.   New England Puritans based their belief on Calvinist theology. Review Calvinist theology from the Reformation and tell how you think that shaped the development of American society. What was Anglicanism, and to what Reformation church did that refer?

2.   In what ways do you think colonial life and government were influenced by the concepts of the Enlightenment that you have studied? Specifically, what thinkers and what ideas were expressed in colonial political organization?

3.   Review mercantilist economic policies that you studied in Chapter 32. How were such policies linked to absolute rulers, and how was the enforcement of mercantilism consistent with colonial policy? How was it inconsistent with colonial beliefs that were so shaped by Enlightenment thought?

4.   The American Revolution became a model for subsequent European revolutions, but those revolutions turned out to be very different and less successful. What elements do you think were unique to the American situation that contributed to the contrast in revolutionary experience?

Chapter 38
The French Revolution, 1789-1799

OVERVIEW

Through the decade of the French Revolution, France experienced great social and political upheavals. This turbulent period marked the turning point into the modern world, and became a symbol for revolutionary aspirations to come.

1. The Last Days of the Old Regime in France. In the late eighteenth century, French society was divided into three orders, or *estates*. People in each estate had hopes and grievances. The first estate was the clergy, prosperous and privileged, although not homogeneous, since priests and monks had more in common with the humble people they served than with rich bishops. The second estate was the nobility, wealthy, exempt from taxation and hoping to gain even more power at the expense of the monarchy. The third estate was the commoners, but this was an extremely heterogeneous group. At the top was the wealthy middle class, eager to take a larger part in political life. There were also urban workers, seeking a decent standard of living. The bottom 90 percent of the population was peasants. They were bound by many old medieval obligations. Above this dissatisfied group was a French government that was arbitrary and inherently unjust.

2. The Breakdown of the Old Regime. Louis XVI had inherited a considerable national debt, and due to inadequate banking and taxation systems, France was in serious financial difficulties. In attempting to resolve the problem, the king confronted vested interests. He called a meeting of the Estates General to try to resolve the financial crisis.

3. The Triumph of the Third Estate. The Third Estate withdrew itself from the Estates General and established a National Assembly to force reform on the French monarchy. With the help of Parisian rioters and peasant revolutionaries, they were able to achieve a guarantee of "natural rights," similar to the Bill of Rights. Although women were excluded from many of the rights, they took charge of forwarding the Revolution by marching on Versailles, taking the king and his family captive and bringing them back to Paris, where the National Assembly become even more radical.

4. Making France A Constitutional Monarchy. The National Assembly drafted a constitution that made France a constitutional monarchy. In addition, the Assembly passed a series of reforms that removed the remnants of medieval society and established the basis of a modern state. Legal, economic, financial, religious and political reforms established Enlightenment principles

and secured, at least for a time, the political influence of the propertied classes.

5.   Foreign War and the Failure of the Moderate Regime. The Constitution of 1791 did not please everyone. Nobility, clergy, and urban workers were not satisfied with it. Further pressure was placed on this constitutional government by the declaration of war on France by the kings of Austria and Prussia, who feared revolutionary momentum. Louis XVI attempted to flee Paris as the Austrian and Prussian armies advanced. He was declared treasonous, giving the radical elements an excuse to call for a new constitution.

6.   The Triumph of the Radicals and the Reign of Terror. Radicals took control of the National Convention that was elected to develop a new constitution to change France from a monarchy to a republic. The National Convention executed the king, causing other European monarchies to join in the war against revolutionary France. To try to bring about a utopian republic in the face of adversity, the radicals introduced a reign of terror during which their perceived enemies were sent to the guillotine. Finally, reaction set in and Robespierre, the radical leader, was executed.

7.   Reaction and the Rise of Napoleon. The propertied middle class, reacting to the excesses of the Reign of Terror, took control of the government, and repealed many of Robespierre's restrictive measures. The National Convention finally drafted a new constitution that reflected the new conservative outlook. The new government was called the Directory, but it was unable to bring order to the country. That would have to wait for Napoleon to take power.

STUDY QUESTIONS

1.   Describe the three estates of French society. What were the privileges and grievances of each? Which groups do you think might join together to gain some of their desires?

2.   What were the economic problems that led Louis XVI to call a meeting of the Estates General? Why couldn't the king and his finance minister resolve the problems?

3.   How was the Estates General converted to a National Assembly that was empowered to revise the French political system? What role did urban workers, peasants and women play in this process?

4.   Describe the judicial, economic, and religious reforms established by the National Assembly in the constitution of 1791. How were these reforms consistent with Enlightenment principles?

5.   What was the political system established in the constitution of 1791? Who had the vote in this constitution, and who did not?

6.   What social groups benefited from the constitution of 1791, and which ones continued to be dissatisfied? What events precipitated the failure of this constitution?

7.   The National Convention that ruled from 1791-1794 brought about more radical reforms than the previous constitution permitted. What were these reforms? Who were the leaders? What did they do to try to bring about their more radical revolution?

8.   What form of government was introduced by the constitution of 1795 after the reaction to the Reign of Terror? Why was this government unable to last and to withstand the coup by Napoleon?

IDENTIFICATION

TRY TO USE EACH OF THESE TERMS AT LEAST ONCE IN ANSWERING THE STUDY QUESTIONS

*Louis XVI	*Great Fear	*"Declaration of
*Estates General	*Civil Constitution of	Rights of Man"
Bastille	the Clergy	*émigré*
*constitution of 1791	J.P. Marat	M. de Robespierre
Jacobin Club	*Reign of Terror	*Thermidorian
*National Convention	*Directory	Reaction
*Napoleon	Turgot	*cahiers*
parlements	*National Assembly	

CHRONOLOGY

List in chronological order the words in the Identification section that have an asterisk (*). As you list these items, put a circle around those that are contemporary.

SAMPLE QUESTIONS

1.   What was the significance of the "Tennis Court Oath"? (Figure 38.1)

2.   Who were the "nobility of the gown"? (p. 493)

3.   What were the problems in the legal system that made it inherently unjust? (p. 494)

4.   Who was Louis XVI's finance minister who attempted to introduce Enlightenment economic reforms, and what were these reforms? (p. 495)

5.   What forced Louis XVI to call a meeting of the Estates General? (p. 495)

6.   What procedural issue made the Third Estate separate and establish a National Assembly? (pp. 495-497)

7.   Under the constitution of 1791, what was the difference between an "active citizen" and a "passive citizen?" (p. 500)

8.   Who were the most radical groups in France who were instrumental in overthrowing the constitution of 1791? (p. 500)

9.   What were the goals of the "Reign of Terror"? (p. 503)

10.   Who was the leader of the Reign of Terror? (p. 503)

11.   The political terms "left" and "right" began in this period. Which term refers to the conservative party? (p. 501)

12.   What was the name of the conservative government established in France as a reaction to the Reign of Terror? (p. 504)

REVIEW AND ANTICIPATION

1.   Compare the plight of the French peasantry on the eve of the Revolution to the position of the peasants in the Middle Ages on the eve of the peasant revolts. How were they the same and how did they differ?

2.   What were some of the grievances that the Third Estate brought to the Estates General? (See "Historians' Sources," p. 496.) Which of these grievances do you think recall the complaints of the Enlightenment thinkers?

3.   The French Revolution will continue to serve as a model and inspire fear among Europeans for the subsequent century or more. What groups do you think will look back at it longingly, and what groups do you think will do everything they can to avoid another such revolution? Are there groups that could feel both impulses?

Chapter 39
The Era of Napoleon, 1799-1815

OVERVIEW

In the chaos of the French Revolution, Napoleon took power and conquered much of Europe. Through his conquest, he spread Enlightenment and revolutionary ideas throughout the Continent.

1. <u>Napoleon's Rise to Power.</u> Napoleon was a brilliant general fighting the countries opposed to the Revolution. His military reputation put him in an excellent position to conspire to take over the government (the Directory) in 1799.

2. <u>The Consulate -- Peace and Reform, 1799-1804.</u> During the first five years of his reign, Napoleon was dramatically successful. He created a constitution that gave him virtually all power, but he used it to bring about and consolidate many reforms that were shaped by the Enlightenment and advocated in the early years of the Revolution. He reformed law codes, ended feudal privileges, affirmed property rights, made peace with the Catholic church while advocating freedom of religion, and stabilized the currency.

3. <u>The Empire -- War and Conquest.</u> Britain feared Napoleon's growing power, and joined with Austria and Russia in 1803 in a coalition against him. Napoleon's land forces seemed to have been invincible, and by 1808 most of continental Europe was under Napoleon's control. British superiority at sea kept Napoleon from being able to attack.

4. <u>Decline and Fall of the Empire.</u> Several things contributed to the downfall of Napoleon's empire: 1) British sea power imposed a blockade on the European continent; 2) the rise of nationalism galvanized opposition to French rule; and 3) Napoleon's disastrous invasion of Russia. The last weakened his seemingly invincible military, so a coalition of forces was able to defeat and exile Napoleon.

5. <u>Overseas Effects: Latin America.</u> Napoleon's conquest of Spain and Portugal reduced their hold over their Latin American colonies. Nationalist independence movements that had been fueled by the writings of the Enlightenment and the examples of the American and French revolutions became so strong that many of the colonies achieved their independence in the 1820s. The former colonies established republics.

6.   <u>The Significance of the French Revolution and Napoleon.</u> The French Revolution and Napoleon introduced a series of ideas and images that profoundly shaped the course of western culture. The ideals of "Liberty, Equality, and Fraternity" became rallying cries for subsequent revolutionaries and political thinkers, and the image of Napoleon as a charismatic leader became a model for some subsequent leaders to imitate.

MAP EXERCISE

See map on p. 174.

1.   In the map of Europe in 1810, write in the following names of countries: Great Britain, Portugal, Spain, France, Austrian Empire, Prussia, Russia, Sweden, Norway, Denmark.

2.   On the same map, identify the following cities: Madrid, Paris, Brussels, Amsterdam, Vienna, Moscow, and Constantinople.

3.   Mark the countries that were either directly controlled by Napoleon or satellite kingdoms. Which were directly hostile in 1810?

4.   The invasion of which country would cause Napoleon to overextend himself and lead ultimately to his downfall? Where is Waterloo, where Napoleon was finally defeated?

STUDY QUESTIONS

1.   How did Napoleon come to power? What in his background prepared him for this opportunity?

2.   What were Napoleon's domestic reforms? (Include his treatment of religion and women, as well as economics and law.) How were they shaped by Enlightenment thought?

3.   Napoleon established his control over most of continental Europe by 1808. How was he able to do so? What country remained outside his control?

4.   What were the three main factors that caused the fall of Napoleon's empire? What finally happened to Napoleon?

5.   How did the Latin American colonies of Spain and Portugal gain their independence? How did Napoleon's rule in Europe speed the cause of Latin American independence movements?

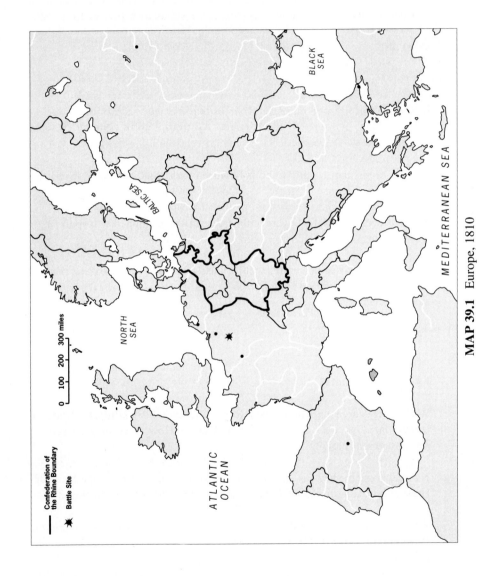

MAP 39.1 Europe, 1810

Confederation of
the Rhine Boundary

Battle Site

BLACK
SEA

MEDITERRANEAN SEA

BALTIC SEA

NORTH
SEA

0 100 200 300 miles

ATLANTIC
OCEAN

6.   The French revolution rallying cry "Liberty, Equality, and Fraternity" offered ideals that people have valued into the modern era. Specifically what goals were embodied in those ideals? How many are still ideals today?

7.   Discuss the various assessments of Napoleon. Was he a great man or a tyrant? What are the arguments on both sides? What do you think?

IDENTIFICATION

TRY TO USE EACH OF THESE TERMS AT LEAST ONCE IN ANSWERING THE STUDY QUESTIONS AND MAP EXERCISES

*consulate	Lord Nelson	Continental System
Alexander I	*Elba	*St. Helena
*Waterloo	Joseph Bonaparte	Simón Bolívar
José San Martín		

CHRONOLOGY

List in chronological order the words in the Identification section that have an asterisk (*). As you list these items, put a circle around those that are contemporary.

SAMPLE QUESTIONS

1.   When Napoleon was fighting the British in Egypt, who won the Battle of the Nile? (p. 506)

2.   What was Napoleon's job in the army? (p. 506)

3.   What did the creation of the Civil Code (the Napoleonic Code) accomplish? (p. 507)

4.   What was the legal position of women in the Napoleonic Code? (p. 507)

5.   Who were Britain's allies against Napoleon in the third coalition in 1803? (p. 508)

6.   What countries were established as satellite kingdoms of Napoleon by 1810? (Map 39.1)

7.   What was the Continental System? (p. 509)

8.   Who were the first people to rebel against the rule of the French? (p. 509)

9.   What invasion was Napoleon's main military error that caused the loss of 500,000 of his troops? (p. 509)

10.   At what battle did Napoleon meet his final defeat? (p. 512)

11.   What was the location of Napoleon's *final* exile? (p. 512)

12.   Who were the leaders of Latin American independence movements? (p. 512)

13.   What kind of law code was introduced in the new free Latin American countries? (p. 513)

REVIEW AND ANTICIPATION

1.   Many enlightened despots wanted to bring about the reforms implemented by Napoleon in his first five years. Why was he able to be successful when they were not?

2.   French rule in Europe caused a growth of nationalism. Can you think of modern examples of how the spirit of nationalism made it impossible for invaders to hold a territory?

3.   With the growth of national spirit that emerged in many European countries after Napoleon's rule, what regions do you think will be motivated to consolidate their nations?

Chapter 40
The Industrial Revolution

OVERVIEW

The Industrial Revolution began in Great Britain in the late eighteenth century and spread all over Europe. It represented a change in economic production that transformed all aspects of life in the West.

1. The Course of the Industrial Revolution. The Industrial Revolution began in Great Britain because of the presence of the right combination of available resources (including capital and workers) and demand for goods. These factors spurred the development of new technology that made Great Britain a leader in industrial production. The technology spread to the Continent after 1830.

2. Technology and Transportation. The Industrial Revolution brought about dramatic changes in technology and transportation. The steam engine provided almost unlimited power to run new machines that mechanized industry (beginning with the cotton textile industry). The factory system required new efficient transportation, and canals, railroads and steam powered ships were developed to satisfy this new demand.

3. The Factory System. Central to the Industrial Revolution was the growth of the factory system in which workers were brought together and trained to produce goods by performing specialized tasks. This system ended the system of domestic manufacturing where artisans would produce goods without supervision. Factories also changed social life by spurring urbanization where workers lived together closely.

4. Social Changes. Industrialization dramatically changed practically all aspects of western life. Population grew and people moved to crowded cities to find work. Urban problems like crime, sanitation, and health increased dramatically. New social classes dominated society. Instead of being structured along traditional lines of nobility and peasantry, the new industrial society was structured on a hierarchy of wealth, with rich middle classes becoming more influential and industrial workers becoming more numerous. Middle-class families became more home-centered with women restricted to and responsible for domestic maintenance. Working-class families also changed -- a demand for labor forced women and children into the poor working conditions of the labor market. Society had to create new solutions to address these sweeping changes.

5.   New Economic and Social Thought. The problems of industrialization brought about various proposals to solve them. The middle class largely adhered to various forms of liberalism, from the extreme laissez-faire policy of total noninvolvement by government in economic issues to limited government intervention as a solution to some of the new problems. More radical solutions were proposed by Utopian Socialists who attempted to establish small societies that were not based on strict competition and which attempted to share the benefits of industrialization more equitably among workers. Most influential was Marxist socialism that proposed a view of history that advocated worker takeover and control of the means of production.

6.   The Arrival of Industrial Society. The changes and problems established by industrialization have shaped the history of the nineteenth-century West.

STUDY QUESTIONS

1.   What combination of assets did Great Britain have that permitted it to be a leader in industrializing production? What prevented nations on the Continent from industrializing until after 1815?

2.   Explain the inventions and other developments that led to the industrialization of the cotton textile industry. Why was the development of new transportation methods crucial to the industrializing process? Have the forms of transportation crucial to modern society changed?

3.   Describe the factory system of production. Do you think workers would get more job satisfaction from domestic cottage industry or factory work? Why? Is modern industry trying to move away from the traditional factory system? Why?

4.   How did the development of the factory system lead to increased urbanization? Is new technology (like computers) changing modern work and living patterns?

5.   Describe the new middle class that was brought to prominence by industrialization. What were its values? What was its family life like? What was the role of middle-class women (be sure to consider the primary document by Elizabeth Poole Sandford)?

6.   Another less privileged class was created by the industrial system, the workers. What were the conditions of their lives? What responses did workers make to their conditions?

7.   By the mid-nineteenth century, government introduced some reforms to improve the conditions of industrial workers. What were some of these reforms? Which of these reforms are still in effect today? What elements of our industrial society still need reform?

8.   Economic liberalism in the nineteenth century advocated a range of government approaches to the problems of industrialization. What were these approaches? Who were the main advocates of each? Which is most similar to today's approaches to government?

9.   What were Utopian Socialists trying to do? How successful were they? Why?

10.   Describe the main elements of Marxist socialism. How was it different from Utopian socialism?

IDENTIFICATION

TRY TO USE EACH OF THESE TERMS AT LEAST ONCE IN ANSWERING THE STUDY QUESTIONS

steam engine	Eli Whitney	James Watt
Robert Fulton	proletariat	bourgeoisie
Molly Maguires	Combination Acts	labor unions
Adam Smith	Thomas Malthus	David Ricardo
Jeremy Bentham	John Stuart Mill	H. de Saint-Simon
Louis Blanc	Robert Owen	Karl Marx
Communist Manifesto	*Das Kapital*	class struggle
Utilitarianism		

SAMPLE QUESTIONS

1.   What specific raw materials did Great Britain have in abundance that helped the beginning of the Industrial Revolution? (p. 516)

2.   The nations on the Continent were in turmoil until after 1815, so they were prevented from industrializing. What was the source of that turmoil? (p. 516)

3.   What were two major industrial cities in England that were adjacent to coal fields? (Map 40.1)

4.   What industry was the first to become mechanized in Great Britain? (p. 517)

5.   Who improved the steam engine so it could be used to drive machinery? (pp. 517-518)

6.   What was the most important new means of transportation that was developed to move industrial goods and materials? (p. 518)

7.   How did industrial capitalists reorganize the process of producing goods under the new industrial system? (pp. 518-519)

8.   Industrialization led to urbanization, but all the people who came to the cities did not work in factories. In what other occupations were people engaged in the cities? (p. 519)

9.   Industrial society replaced the old social classes of aristocracy and peasantry with new classes. What were they? (p. 520)

10.   What in Thomas Malthus' theory suggested that nothing can be done to improve the lot of the masses? (p. 525)

11.   What political theorist was one of the first to advocate equal rights for women? (p. 526)

12.   What political theorists attacked the unregulated pursuit of profits? (p. 527)

13.   What is "surplus value" according to Karl Marx? (p. 528)

14.   Would Karl Marx have supported nationalism as an ideal? (p. 528)

REVIEW AND ANTICIPATION

1.   Review the agricultural revolution and the growth of cottage industries. How did these developments aid the development of the Industrial Revolution in Great Britain?

2.   When you consider conditions faced by industrial workers, how do you think they will respond? What do you think will be the most effective means of correcting the hardships and inequities of the industrial system?

3.   Before Marxist communism is implemented in Europe in the twentieth century, it will undergo some transformation. What do you think will be changed before it can be imposed?

Chapter 41
Romanticism in Philosophy, Literature, and the Arts

OVERVIEW

In the nineteenth century a new cultural style became pervasive in the West. This style influenced literature, philosophy and the arts and continues to exert an influence today.

1.   The Nature of Romanticism. The romantic spirit represented a reaction against the rationalism that had preceded it. Romantics valued emotion and feeling over understanding laws of nature. Romantics also embraced nationalism, emotional religiosity, and a study of history (especially medieval) as ways to feel the truth of the human spirit.

2.   The Philosophy of Idealism. Some philosophers rejected the emphasis on reason that had dominated the Enlightenment. Rousseau stressed feeling, emotions, and love of nature. Kant believed that faith and feeling were the only ways to have access to spiritual truth. This approach to truth has come to be known as the philosophy of idealism. Hegel developed an understanding of history that rejected the amoral universe of the Enlightenment.

3.   Romantic Literature. Poetry and prose that expressed the values of romanticism flourished in Europe and America throughout the nineteenth century.

4.   The Romantic Spirit in the Arts. The ideals of romanticism were expressed in the visual arts as well. Painters created works that appealed to the emotions. Architects revived the medieval Gothic style, and musicians expressed national spirit in works designed to appeal to the emotions rather than the intellect.

STUDY QUESTIONS

1.   What were the characteristics of romanticism? Name at least one romantic figure that expresses each of the characteristics.

2.   Explain the philosophy of idealism as expressed by Rousseau and Kant. How does this philosophy contrast with the principles of the Enlightenment?

3.   What was Hegel's view of how history progresses?

4.   Which romantic authors would you say best express a profound love of nature? Which express a mystic religious feeling? Which express a love of nationalism by writing about the medieval history of their country?

5.   What themes did the leading romantic painters glorify? Give examples of some of the painters. Look at the paintings illustrated in the text. Describe the romantic characteristics visible in each painting.

6.   Who were the major romantic composers? What were they trying to accomplish in their works?

IDENTIFICATION

TRY TO USE EACH OF THESE TERMS AT LEAST ONCE IN ANSWERING THE STUDY QUESTIONS

Lord Byron	*zeitgeist*	S.T. Coleridge
T.B. Macaulay	Alexander Dumas	H.D. Thoreau
Immanuel Kant	Alexander Pushkin	Beethoven
F. Schleiermacher	Sir Walter Scott	Richard Wagner
Jules Michelet	Rousseau	dialectical system
G.W. Hegel	Edgar Allan Poe	Robert Burns
Critique of Pure	George Sand	J.W. von Goethe
Reason	M.W. Turner	Franz List
William Wordsworth	Frédéric Chopin	J.F. Millet
H. Heine	Victor Hugo	

SAMPLE QUESTIONS

1.   Lord Byron's death revealed one aspect of romanticism. How did he die? (p. 531)

2.   Romantics rejected deism in favor of what religious emphasis? (p. 531)

3.   Love of nationalism caused romantics to favor one particular period of history. What was it? (p. 531)

4.   What did Hegel believe dominated each historical epoch? (p. 532)

5.   What kinds of truths did Kant believe could not be proven by reason? (p. 532)

6.   Who advocated the notion that every historical epoch is dominated by a particular spirit of the time? (p. 532)

7.   What is a dialectical system? (p. 532)

8.   What poets dignified and popularized romanticism in Great Britain? (p. 533)

9.   What Scottish poet idealized nature and the rustic rural life? (p. 533)

10.   Who wrote *Faust*, and what is its basic theme? (p. 534)

11.   How was the romantic movement expressed in architecture? (p. 535)

12.   What German romantic composer is known for stridently nationalistic music, particularly opera? (p. 537)

REVIEW AND ANTICIPATION

1.   Reconsider the principles of the Enlightenment. Contrast those with the ideals of romanticism. Which do you think most fully expresses the truth of human experience?

2.   The romantics looked to the Middle Ages as an ideal time for recapturing a national spirit. From what you studied about medieval times, do you think they were accurate or were they looking to an imagined world?

3.   Romanticism remains a strong force in Western civilization into the twentieth century. Can you think of ways that romanticism might influence political movements?

Chapter 42
Conservatism, Restoration, and Reaction, 1815-1830

OVERVIEW

After the fall of Napoleon, aristocrats restored order to European society, and attempted to hold on to this order by conservative ideology and repressive techniques.

1.   The Congress of Vienna, 1814-1815. After the defeat of Napoleon, the major victors assembled in Vienna to restore Europe. They were governed by conservative ideology and adhered to the principles of legitimacy and stability in their decisions regarding the map of Europe. In their settlements, they attempted to keep a balance of power in Europe, rather than punish France for the Revolution. While the congress neglected new forces of liberalism and nationalism, it did introduce a century-long period that was free from Europe-wide war.

2.   The Concert of Europe. The members of the Congress of Vienna attempted to set up mechanisms for preserving the settlement. They formed alliances and sent armies into countries in which there were revolts against the order established in Vienna. Splits, however, did appear in the alliances. Great Britain repudiated the system, the United States challenged European interference in the New World, and the Greek struggle for independence galvanized sympathy. Europe was not to act in concert for long.

3.   The Bourbon Restoration in France. Consistent with the principle of legitimacy, a younger brother of the guillotined Louis XVI was placed on the throne. This "restored" member of the Bourbon family was moderate and careful not to alienate those who had benefited from Napoleon's rule. His brother, Charles X, however, was not so cautious. When he took the throne, he attempted to make France more conservative. The Parisians revolted and exiled this last Bourbon king.

4.   Restoration and Repression in the Germanies. The Germanies in 1815 consisted of thirty-seven small states and Austria and Prussia. Austria and Prussia were extremely conservative (also called reactionary) and they introduced repressive measures to be sure that no liberal or nationalist impulses would threaten the status quo. Austria was particularly worried about nationalism since its empire was made up of varied peoples.

5.   Restoration and Repression in Italy. In Austria and Austria-dominated regions of Italy, the deposed aristocracy returned with a vengeance and

eliminated all of Napoleon's reforms and persecuted those who disagreed with their conservative position.

6.   Conservatism in Great Britain. Even Great Britain, with its democratic tradition, had a very conservative government. Only about 5 percent of adult males could vote, and politics was dominated by the conservative Tory party. By 1822, the government loosened its controls a bit, but pressure to increase participation in government by extending the vote intensified.

7.   Reaction and Repression in Russia. Although some of the Russian aristocracy had been exposed to liberal and romantic ideas, such views had little chance to flourish in a land dominated by a feudal agricultural system and a conservative Orthodox Christian church. Czar Nicholas I vigorously put down revolts advocating liberal reforms.

8.   Conservatism and the Challenge of Liberalism. Under Metternich's system, it appeared that conservative ideology favoring a Christian, hierarchic society would prevail. Yet, the political forces that were expressed in liberal ideals would continue to challenge this order.

MAP EXERCISE

See map on p. 186.

1.   Look at the extent of the Austrian Empire. What Italian states are nearest to that empire and most likely to fall under its influence?

2.   Locate Poland. What states surround and threaten it? Poland has no seaport on this map. What state would have to lose territory if Poland were to achieve this important economic entity of ready access to the sea?

3.   What German states would Prussia have to take to make its territory solidly joined?

4.   Locate Gibraltar. Why is it strategically so important?

STUDY QUESTIONS

1.   What were the goals of the Congress of Vienna? Who attended? What principles guided their deliberations, and how successful were their resolutions? What did they mean by "legitimacy" and "stability"?

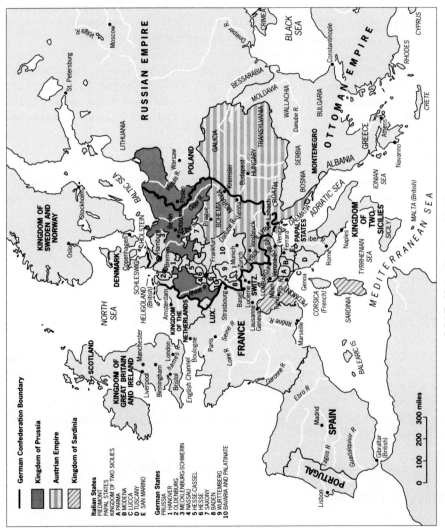

MAP 42.1 Europe, 1815

German Confederation Boundary

Kingdom of Prussia

Austrian Empire

Kingdom of Sardinia

Italian States
PIEDMONT
PAPAL STATES
KINGDOM OF TWO SICILIES
A PARMA
B MODENA
C LUCCA
D TUSCANY
E SAN MARINO

German States
PRUSSIA
1 HANOVER
2 OLDENBURG
3 MECKLENBURG-SCHWERIN
4 NASSAU
5 HESSE-CASSEL
6 HESSE
7 SAXONY
8 BADEN
9 WÜRTTEMBERG
10 BAVARIA AND PALATINATE

0 100 200 300 miles

2.   Describe the nineteenth-century conservative ideology. Who was the main proponent? How is it different from our modern American conservative party?

3.   What alliances were formed to try to implement the settlement of the Congress of Vienna? Which was the most effective? What got in the way of the alliances acting together?

4.   What was the differing policy between the two Bourbon kings, Louis XVIII and Charles X? Which was more successful? Why?

5.   German nationalist movements appeared in small states in Germany. Discuss these movements and tell how they were suppressed.

6.   Discuss the tension between conservative and liberal forces in Great Britain in the early nineteenth century. Which parties represented which side? How did the law of primogeniture help to bring about a mingling between upper and middle classes?

7.   Prussia, Russia and Austria were the most conservative countries. What did they have in common that might lead to this political stance? What differences did they have?

IDENTIFICATION

TRY TO USE EACH OF THESE TERMS AT LEAST ONCE IN ANSWERING THE STUDY QUESTIONS AND MAP EXERCISES

Congress of Vienna	Lord Castlereagh	Frederick William III
Alexander I	Metternich	Holy Alliance
Talleyrand	Edmund Burke	Treaty of Adrianople
Quadruple Alliance	Monroe Doctrine	*Burschenschaften*
Louis XVIII	Charles X	Peterloo Massacre
Hapsburgs	Hohenzollerns	
Tory	Whig	
Nicholas I		

SAMPLE QUESTIONS

1.   Who did the nineteenth-century conservatives believe should rule society? (p. 540)

2.   Napoleon had destroyed the Holy Roman Empire. What did the Congress of Vienna erect in its place? (p. 541)

3.   Who were the members of the Quadruple Alliance? (p. 543)

4.   Who was the first of the great powers to repudiate the Metternich system? (p. 543)

5.   What kept the Holy Alliance from interfering in the Western Hemisphere? (p. 543)

6.   What was the result of the Greek war of independence? (p. 544)

7.   Which of Napoleon's reforms did Louis XVIII keep? (p. 544)

8.   What was the name of the dynasty that was restored to the French throne after the fall of Napoleon? (p. 544)

9.   What French king ended up in exile after the Parisians rioted against his rule? (pp. 544-545)

10.   In which German states were nationalism and liberalism most promoted? (p. 545)

11.   What were the *Burschenschaften*? (p. 545)

12.   What were the reactionary (conservative) landed aristocracy in Prussia called and why were they influential? (p. 545)

13.   What were the two most reactionary states in Europe? (p. 546)

14.   Because of the suffrage laws in Great Britain, who monopolized both houses of Parliament? (p. 546)

15.   What issues led to the Peterloo Massacre? (p. 547)

16.   What Czar vigorously suppressed revolts against any liberal reforms? (p. 548)

REVIEW AND ANTICIPATION

1.   In Chapter 40, you read about political ideas that grew up in response to the industrial challenges faced by nineteenth-century society. How would the conservative position address those same issues?

2.   Look at the map in your text (Map 42.1) of Europe in 1815. What territory do you think Prussia will want to acquire as it increasingly feels nationalistic impulses?

3.   The Austrian Empire was worried about all the nationalities within its border. Do you think this will continue to be a cause of instability in this region? Are states with many nationalities inherently unstable? Are there modern examples of this?

Chapter 43
Liberalism and Revolution, 1830-1850

OVERVIEW

    Between 1830-1850, liberal reforms swept through Europe, sometimes peacefully and sometimes by revolution. While they did not succeed in completely replacing old entrenched power, they did make some changes that point to future European political developments.

1.   <u>The General Nature of Nineteenth-Century Liberalism.</u> In contrast to the conservative ideology that reigned after the defeat of Napoleon, liberal political thought flowered after 1830. Nineteenth-century liberals believed in individualism, and that government should be limited in order to strengthen the rights and freedoms of individuals. Liberals also believed in the power of reason and in the right of rational (propertied) people to govern. The increasingly important middle class tended to support liberalism.

2.   <u>Political and Social Reform in Great Britain.</u> The Reform Bill of 1832 broadened the suffrage in Britain and marked a turning point in British history that moved that country toward liberalism. The House of Commons demonstrated its superiority over the House of Lords and many liberal reforms were introduced. These reforms primarily addressed the interests of the middle class, but urban workers, too, had an agenda they advocated in the Chartist movement. The political parties became aware of these demands and eventually would enact many of them into law.

3.   <u>Liberal Revolutions in Belgium and France.</u> The conservative plan that forced Belgium and the Netherlands to join failed in 1830. Belgians revolted and achieved their independence from the Dutch and adopted a liberal constitution. In France, too, the conservative monarchy of Charles X had fallen. A new monarchy was established with a king who believed in the power of the middle class and endorsed many liberal reforms, but he neglected the aspirations of the working classes.

4.   <u>The Revolution of 1848 in France.</u> In 1848, the working classes in Paris began a revolution against the liberal government that had neglected them. The king went into exile and a socialist government that was based on universal male suffrage and the right to work in national workshops was established. However, property owners (including peasants) feared this radical threat to property and in the election of 1848 voted in a more conservative government. The first president was a nephew of Napoleon, who ultimately destroyed the constitution and took complete power.

5.   The Revolution of 1848 in Central Europe. In the German lands and Austria, revolutionaries stressed nationalism in addition to the desire for liberal reforms. At first it appeared that the Austrian emperor would be forced to introduce liberal reforms and perhaps even offer national sovereignty to non-German nationalities within its borders. However, with the help of Russia, Austria was able to suppress the revolutionaries, as did Prussia.

6.   Revolution in Italy. Revolutions broke out in Italy that had the goals of liberalism and nationalism. While some states adopted liberal constitutions, Austrian intervention was able to suppress the revolts and delay national unification.

7.   An Assessment. The revolutions from 1830-1848 did bring about a number of liberal reforms in various countries. But, by 1850 conservative forces had regained some control. People advocating revolutionary agenda could not all agree on what changes should be brought about, so the more cohesive conservative forces were able to prevail over many liberal reforms.

MAP EXERCISE

See map on p. 192.

1.   On this map of Europe, mark the sites of some of the revolts that took place between 1820 and 1848. Indicate at least ten.

2.   Which country/region had the most revolts? Which countries might have felt most threatened by the revolts in neighboring countries?

3.   Which countries interfered in the revolts in other countries?

4.   Notice the location of the newly separated Belgium and the Netherlands. Which country do you think will have most interest in the affairs of Belgium?

STUDY QUESTIONS

1.   Describe nineteenth-century liberalism. Include their opinions on government, individual rights, economics, and religion.

2.   What was the impact in Britain of the Reform Bill of 1832? (Include the impact on suffrage and on the existing political parties.) List some liberal reforms that were passed after that time.

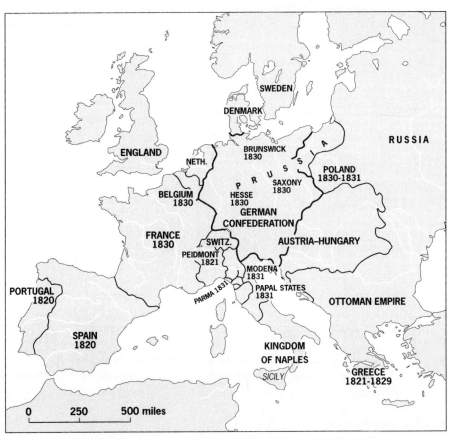

MAP 43.1 European Revolts, 1820–1831 and 1848–1849

3.   What were the demands of the Chartist movement in Britain? How would these demands specifically address the needs of working people instead of propertied middle class people? Which of these demands are in place in our society today?

4.   What were the differences between Belgium and the Netherlands that caused Belgium to revolt for independence? Are there countries today that are stressed by similar pressures?

5.   Who was the "bourgeois monarch" of France who replaced the conservative Charles X? What policies did he follow that earned him that title? What group did he neglect that led to the revolutions of 1848?

6.   What were the goals of the French revolutionaries of 1848? What did they accomplish? Who took over the government after the collapse of the revolution?

7.   How were the revolutions in 1848 in Central Europe and Italy different from that in France? What was the result of these revolutions? What countries intervened to suppress these revolts?

8.   By 1850, conservative forces were again in the ascendancy. What factors accounted for the defeat of liberal and nationalist forces? Do you think these issues are permanently defeated?

IDENTIFICATION

TRY TO USE EACH OF THESE TERMS AT LEAST ONCE IN ANSWERING THE STUDY QUESTIONS AND MAP EXERCISES

Whigs	Louis Philippe	*Carbonari*
Chartist movement	Reform Bill of 1832	Frederick William IV
Tories	G. Mazzini	Metternich
Louis Napoleon	"June Days"	Louis Blanc
Bonaparte	Hapsburg	Hohenzollern
Ferdinand I		

SAMPLE QUESTIONS

1.   What is the role of government in the ideology of nineteenth-century liberalism? (p. 551)

2.   During the first half of the nineteenth century, liberals believed that who should have the right to vote? (p. 551)

3.   From what social group did liberals usually come? (p. 551)

4.   In Britain in the 1830s the Whig party changed its name to reflect its new political ideology. What was the new name? (p. 553)

5.   What were some of the regulations that limited child and female labor in Britain after 1833? (p. 553)

6.   What movement demanded universal male suffrage and secret ballot? (p. 554)

7.   What religion was predominant in Belgium? What was predominant in the Netherlands? (p. 554)

8.   What king was brought to power by the July Revolution in France? (p. 555)

9.   After the revolution of 1848 in France, what did the socialists establish to try to help the urban workers? (p. 556)

10.   Who was elected president of the Second French Republic in 1848 by the vote of all adult males? (p. 556)

11.   In central Europe the revolutions for liberalism were entwined with what other agenda? (p. 557)

12.   What was the center of revolution in central Europe? (p. 557)

13.   What country helped the Austrians suppress the revolts in Austria and Hungary? (p. 558)

14.   Who was the leader of the Young Italy society that was dedicated to achieving a united Italy? (p. 558)

15.   What country intervened in Italy to crush the revolutions of 1848? (p. 559)

REVIEW AND ANTICIPATION

1.   Reconsider the values of the Enlightenment and of romanticism. What elements from each form parts of liberal ideology? In general, which of these is most consistent with nineteenth-century liberalism?

2.   The Hapsburg Empire almost fell apart along national (language group) lines in 1848. Do you think that will remain a problem in that region? Is it a problem today?

3.   Do you expect the movements for national unification that took place in Germany and Italy to subside?

4.   Do you think the political beliefs of liberalism and nationalism will challenge organized religion?

Chapter 44
Nationalism and the Nation-State,
1850-1871

OVERVIEW

Between 1850-1871 nationalism became a dominant force in western political life, and was embraced by both liberals and conservatives.

1. <u>The Nature of Nationalism.</u> Before the French Revolution, national loyalty usually meant loyalty to one's monarch. Afterwards, nationalism became tied to other things. Most important was language, although other factors such as historical traditions of unity or religion also made an impact.

2. <u>The Second Empire of Napoleon III.</u> Louis Napoleon, the elected president of the French republic, organized a coup d'état and had himself declared the hereditary emperor -- Napoleon III. While his regime was quite autocratic, he granted many liberal reforms that were designed to please many varied groups in his country. His internal policies made him popular and France prosperous. He reached the height of his prestige during the Crimean War, in which France was victorious against Russia. However, other foreign policy adventures were less successful. He attempted to conquer and control Mexico, and finally was defeated in a war against Germany during which his government was overthrown.

3. <u>Cavour and the Making of Italian Unity.</u> The prime minister of the Italian state of Piedmont-Sardinia, Cavour, was able to use wise diplomacy and careful warfare to unify the Italian states under the leadership of the constitutional monarchy of Piedmont. Most of the northern states joined Piedmont bloodlessly, and Garibaldi invaded the south with a very small army. Popular sentiment allowed him to sweep north until he turned over the south to the king of Piedmont-Sardinia. Italy was unified.

4. <u>German Unification.</u> The Prussian chancellor, von Bismarck, used nationalism and military victory to suppress liberalism in Prussia and to unify the German states under Prussian leadership. Germany was unified primarily through warfare. Prussia first fought Austria and took over Austria's control of the German confederation. Prussia then fought a successful war against France. The government of Napoleon III fell and a new French republic was declared. The Prussian king William I was crowned emperor of the German Empire, and a new dominant power had been introduced into Europe.

MAP EXERCISE

See map on p. 198.

1. On the map of Italy, locate the following: Piedmont, Tuscany, Papal States, Sicily, Kingdom of Naples, Sardinia, Rome.

2. Notice from the key how few years it took to unite all these states. Why didn't it take longer?

3. Locate Austria. Why was Austria always so interested in what was going on in Italy?

4. Notice the old Papal States. Why would some Roman Catholics in Italy have objected to the unification?

STUDY QUESTIONS

1. What elements contribute to feelings of common cultural identity that we call nationalism? Do those factors still define our nations today?

2. In his domestic affairs, Napoleon III of France wisely introduced policies that would appeal to varied social groups. What were these policies, and to whom would each appeal?

3. Describe Napoleon III's foreign policies. Which were successful, and which were not? Why do you think he became involved in so many other countries when he was so successful domestically?

4. Describe the process by which Italy was unified. Who were the leaders? How did they achieve their goal? What form of government was introduced in the newly unified country?

5. How was Germany unified under Prussia's rule? Contrast German unification with that of Italy. Who were the leaders of the German unification?

6. How did Bismarck use nationalism against liberalism? Why was Bismarck called the "Iron Chancellor"? Do you think military victories will still make people forget their rights?

7. What was the result of the Franco-Prussian war?

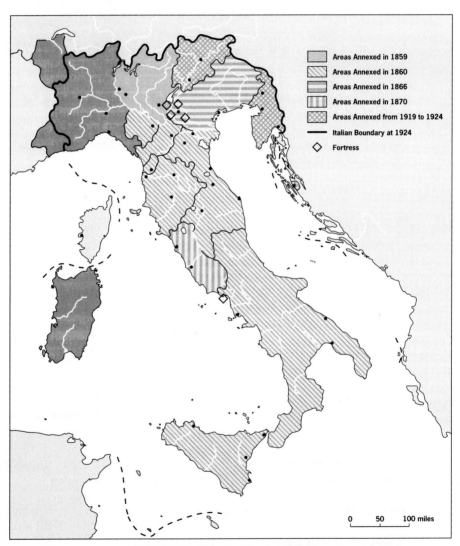

Areas Annexed in 1859
Areas Annexed in 1860
Areas Annexed in 1866
Areas Annexed in 1870
Areas Annexed from 1919 to 1924
Italian Boundary at 1924
Fortress

0   50   100 miles

MAP 44.1 The Unification of Italy

IDENTIFICATION

TRY TO USE EACH OF THESE TERMS AT LEAST ONCE IN ANSWERING
THE STUDY QUESTIONS AND MAP EXERCISES

Napoleon III	Crimean War	Florence
Maximilian	Nicholas I	Nightingale
Cavour	Victor Emmanuel	G. Garibaldi
William I	von Bismarck	"Iron Chancellor"
Treaty of Prague	Treaty of Frankfurt	

SAMPLE QUESTIONS

1.   What is the most important factor in defining one's nationality? (p. 562)

2.   Until the French Revolution, how was national loyalty chiefly defined? (p. 562)

3.   How did Napoleon III become Emperor of France? (p. 562)

4.   How did Napoleon III encourage industrialization and economic growth? (p. 563)

5.   What was the issue that precipitated the Crimean War? (p. 564)

6.   What was the relationship between Maximilian of Mexico and Napoleon III? (p. 564)

7.   Who helped inspire the creation of the International Red Cross after the Crimean War? (p. 564)

8.   What benefit did Piedmont gain by supporting France in the Crimean War? (p. 566)

9.   Who conquered the Kingdom of Naples in order to help unify Italy? (p. 566)

10.   Who was the king of the newly declared Kingdom of Italy in 1861? (p. 566)

11.   What German states were annexed by Prussia in 1866 that joined the two separate parts of Prussia together? (Map 44.2)

12.   How did the new Kingdom of Italy incorporate the state of Venetia (Venice)? (p. 570)

13.   What did Germany gain in the Franco-Prussian War? (p. 571)

14.   What form of government was introduced into France after the fall of Napoleon III? (p. 571)

REVIEW AND ANTICIPATION

1.   Review the revolutionary issues from 1848. How many continued to be in the forefront during these wars of the late nineteenth century? What do you think happened to the rest of the grievances? Are they permanently gone?

2.   Prussia's military successes show the power of nationalism combined with militarism. What countries do you expect to continue that policy? Will it be most likely the winners of these wars or the losers?

Chapter 45
Industrial Society, Social Classes,
and Women

OVERVIEW

By the late nineteenth century, industrial society had come of age. The West was dominated by an urban, industrial society with a class system based on wealth and work. New products and processes brought increasing wealth, and women were beginning to insist upon access to the political process.

1.   The Second Industrial Revolution. In the last third of the nineteenth century, the "second Industrial Revolution" was initiated. This revolution was based on electricity, oil, steel, and chemicals: new products and processes that spurred an upsurge of industrial production particularly in the United States and Germany, which quickly surpassed Great Britain in industrial production. As part of this upsurge, the development of the automobile and airplane pointed to a future not linked to rail and water. Communications were speeded by the development of telegraph, telephone and radio. The wealth generated by these improvements was frequently centered in giant corporations and monopolies.

2.   The Rise of Working-Class Organizations and Ideologies. By the late nineteenth century, industrial workers became a significant political force. Workers banded together in labor unions that increasingly could influence political decisions. In addition, they formed cooperatives that offered much-needed fellowship of workers. The major ideological force within the working class was socialism, and Marx offered the most influential socialist model. Some Marxists were moderate, arguing that revolution was not necessary, and others continued to advocate revolution. Socialists in all countries became more numerous. Anarchists advocated elimination of all authority.

3.   The Growth and Movement of Population. The population of Europe exploded throughout the nineteenth century, and it was fueled mostly by reduced death rates because birth rates were falling. This population was also highly mobile; millions of people emigrated to the New World, and just as many moved from the countryside to urban areas. As a result, cities became a focus of attention and planning and were designed to be more pleasant places to live than they had been before.

4.   Social Classes. There was much prosperity in late nineteenth-century Europe and the wealth continued to be divided among classes. The middle class

continued to advocate a strict work ethic, and after 1848 ceased to be a revolutionary force, preferring to preserve the status quo. Professionals and white-collar workers joined middle-class ranks, and all aspired to imitate the lifestyles of those wealthier than they. Some members of the working class, too, were becoming a bit more prosperous, with time to enjoy some leisure activities. However, the gap between rich and poor remained wide.

5.   <u>Women's Roles and Experiences.</u> While there was a great deal of diversity between women's experiences along class lines, nevertheless, all women shared a lack of political rights, economic dependence, and social restrictions. Middle-class women were responsible for caring for the home, and only late in the nineteenth century were some professions open to them. Working-class women were likely to work outside the home, but their wages were much lower than those of their male counterparts. Increasingly women's organizations advocated political rights and freedoms, but in most places women would have to wait until the turn of the century to achieve a measure of sovereignty.

STUDY QUESTIONS

1.   The second Industrial Revolution marked a change from the first. What new products and processes were developed? How did these spur a new surge of growth? How were these new products linked to new possibilities in transportation?

2.   What new means of communication were developed in the late nineteenth century? How do you think these will lead to more rapid changes?

3.   How did pure science begin increasingly to make an impact on industry? What fields contributed most to the second Industrial Revolution?

4.   Describe the process by which labor unions gained legitimacy in the West. What are cooperatives, and how did they benefit workers? To what degree are labor unions and cooperatives significant forces for workers today?

5.   How did socialism become a political force in the late nineteenth century? What were the differing approaches to implementing socialism? How is socialism different from anarchism?

6.   The growing population of industrial Europe was becoming more mobile in the nineteenth century. Where did people move? Why? What were the results of all this movement on society?

7. Describe the social classes that made up late nineteenth-century society. What values did they hold? What were their aspirations? What were their leisure activities?

8. Discuss the roles of women in nineteenth-century society. Be sure to compare and contrast middle-class women's experiences with those of working-class women. What efforts did women make in the late nineteenth century to bring about reform? How successful were these efforts?

IDENTIFICATION

TRY TO USE EACH OF THESE TERMS AT LEAST ONCE IN ANSWERING THE STUDY QUESTIONS

Bessemer process	M. Faraday	T.A. Edison
Gottlieb Daimler	Henry Ford	A.G. Bell
G. Marconi	Karl Marx	Labour Party
First International	Second International	E. Bernstein
Fabian Society	E. Pankhurst	R. Luxemburg
anarchism		

SAMPLE QUESTIONS

1. What products formed the basis for the second Industrial Revolution? (p. 575)

2. What countries took the lead in industrialization away from Great Britain in the late nineteenth century? (p. 575)

3. Who developed the first practical internal combustion engine? (p. 576)

4. Who first applied the assembly-line method of mass production to automobiles, making them more affordable? (p. 577)

5. With what political party in Britain were the labor unions associated? (p. 578)

6. What was the First International? (p. 578)

7. Who modified Marx's theory and argued that revolution would not be necessary to introduce socialism? (p. 579)

8. In what country did socialism have its greatest success before 1914? (p. 579)

9.   What do anarchists advocate? (p. 579)

10.   By the turn of the century, what percent of the population in western Europe lived in urban areas? (p. 580)

11.   Who were the most important new groups to join the middle class? (p. 582)

12.   What were some of the leisure-time activities engaged in by the working classes? (p. 582)

13.   What was the main issue for nineteenth-century feminists? (p. 584)

REVIEW AND ANTICIPATION

1.   What industry and processes was the first Industrial Revolution based on?

2.   Monopolies dominated the second Industrial Revolution. Do you think monopolies are consistent with the laissez-faire capitalism that was advocated by Enlightenment thinkers, or do you think monopolies will be controlled in the name of free enterprise?

3.   The book indicates that women increasingly got the vote after World War I. Why do you think the experience of war would help women get the vote when it was denied them in the nineteenth century?

Chapter 46
Science and the Challenge to Christianity

OVERVIEW

The discoveries of the late nineteenth century fueled an optimism in people's abilities to understand the secrets of the world. Such scientific discoveries and other modern views challenged many traditional religious beliefs.

1.   The Physical, Biological, and Medical Sciences. There were many advances in the field of physical sciences in the late nineteenth century. Understanding of the atomic structure of matter was forwarded and Albert Einstein revolutionized physics with his theories of mass and energy and relativity. In the biological sciences, Darwin developed the theory of evolution, which was applied to society by some philosophers. In medicine, researchers increased knowledge of anatomy and discovered bacteria, which opened the way for dramatic improvements in health. The new science continued to be dominated by men, since women were excluded.

2.   The Rise of Social Science. Scientific techniques were applied to the study of humans and society, creating new disciplines and insights. Studies of the human mind led to discoveries of the importance of reflexes, and led to Freud's influential discoveries of the power of the unconscious. Sociology was developed to understand laws of human society, and historians were striving to make the study of history scientific. All these developments contributed to an optimistic belief in progress.

3.   Challenges to Christianity. The developments of the nineteenth century seemed to challenge Christian faith and practices. The dislocations of industrialization undermined traditional Christian practices. Liberal political movements challenged traditional organized churches that frequently aligned with conservatives, and liberal reforms removed education from clerical control. Nationalism, too, seemed to challenge international allegiances to a Christian church. Finally, progress in science itself challenged old beliefs. Theories of evolution, positivism, psychology, social sciences, and even Biblical criticism raised doubts about old beliefs.

4.   The Christian Response. There were three main Christian reactions to the challenges posed by new ideas. The first was angry rejection in which new ideas were forbidden. The second reaction was to surrender to the critique and go through the motions of faith without really believing. The third reaction was the Church's acceptance of the new scientific beliefs and attempting to make them compatible with faith.

STUDY QUESTIONS

1.   Describe the nineteenth-century discoveries in the physical sciences that led to our understanding of the makeup of the material world. Do you agree that this model could lead to feelings that the material world seemed less solid and reliable?

2.   Describe the theory of evolution. Would this theory also lead to questioning traditional understandings of humanity?

3.   What were the most important advances in medicine in the late nineteenth century?

4.   Describe the nineteenth-century discoveries in the field of psychology. Be sure to explain the theory of Freud. Which of these discoveries continue to be powerful today?

5.   What was Comte's theory? How did his belief in the "positive" age reflect the ideals of optimism in science? How did his beliefs undermine religious values?

6.   Describe how industrialization and the growth of the new political ideas of liberalism and nationalism served to raise questions about traditional Christian belief. Do you think these differences are irreconcilable?

7.   Describe how new scientific ideas in the biological and social sciences served to raise questions about traditional Christian belief.

8.   Explain the three ways churches reacted to the challenge posed by the new ideas of the nineteenth century. Which do you think was most effective? Do such conflicts in conscience occur today? How do people respond today?

9.   Pope Leo XIII addressed the new problems raised by industrialization. What did he proclaim as the Church's position on the new industrial life?

IDENTIFICATION

TRY TO USE EACH OF THESE TERMS AT LEAST ONCE IN ANSWERING THE STUDY QUESTIONS

D. Mendeléev	Auguste Comte	H. Spencer
Charles Darwin	Zionism	Joseph Lister
Louis Pasteur	modernists	Sigmund Freud
Ivan Pavlov	A. Einstein	positivism

James Frazer	relativity	*Rerum Novarum*
Pope Leo XIII	E = mc²	*Syllabus of Errors*
	On the Origin of the	L. von Ranke
	Species	psychoanalysis

SAMPLE QUESTIONS

1.   Mendeléev worked out a chart that organized all the elements. What was the basis for this organization? (p. 587)

2.   What is the essence of Einstein's theory of relativity? (p. 587)

3.   What did Darwin believe determined changes in animal characteristics? (p. 588)

4.   What discovery made surgery relatively safe for the first time in history? (p. 589)

5.   What was the implication of Pavlov's experiments for human behavior? (p. 589)

6.   What did Freud conclude was the proper therapy for neuroses? (p. 590)

7.   What is positivism? (p. 590)

8.   What historian strove to make the study of history a science? (p. 590)

9.   What theory caused the greatest conflict between natural science and Christian religion? (p. 591)

10.   How did anthropologists undermine belief in religion? (p. 592)

11.   What was the doctrine of papal infallibility? (p. 592)

12.   What would people who considered themselves "modernists" have believed about the Bible and Christ? (p. 593)

13.   What was Pope Leo XIII's position on evolution? (p. 593)

14.   What permitted the growth of Roman Catholic labor unions? (p. 594)

REVIEW AND ANTICIPATION

1.   Review the ideas of the Scientific Revolution and the Enlightenment. Do the developments in the late nineteenth century reveal the continued power of these ideas? How?

2.   What was Thomas Aquinas attempting to do in his synthesis of knowledge, the *Summa Theologica*? How was that consistent with Pope Leo XIII's reconciliation between faith and science? What was different about Aquinas' attempts?

3.   What scientific developments do you think will have the most impact in the decades to follow?

Chapter 47
Thought and Culture in an Age of
Nationalism and Industrialization

OVERVIEW

During the second half of the nineteenth century, the thought and art of the age increasingly moved away from romanticism into an era of realism, in which artists criticized middle-class values and inserted pessimism and introspection into western culture.

1. Popular Education, Journalism, and Culture. In the late nineteenth century, societies had a growing commitment to public education, and as a result, illiteracy almost disappeared from the West by 1914. The rise in literacy was accompanied by a growth in popular newspapers that not only brought information to the public, but promoted the views of the powerful corporations that bought advertising. In addition, there was a growth in other forms of entertainment for popular tastes. Pulp fiction, popular music and commercial films became increasingly prevalent.

2. Currents of Thought: Nationalism, Racism, and Disenchantment. The strong nationalism of the nineteenth century was increasingly reflected in racism and a growing militarism. Some thinkers began to confuse the notion of "race" with language groupings and argued for a hierarchy that valued some "races" over others. Other philosophers took a pessimistic view of the struggle for life and argued for will, power, and practicality as the only real truths. These ideas revealed a dark side of nineteenth-century thought.

3. Realistic Literature. Realistic literature, expressed most generally in novels and drama, reflected the materialism, cynicism and pessimism of the late industrial age. It was influenced by the "realism" of Darwin and Freud and held a mirror to the mundane and dark side of industrial life.

4. Impressionist and Modern Painting and Sculpture. Visual artists reacted against old forms of art much as realistic novelists did. Impressionist painters drew from the scientific study of color and light to create paintings in suggestive shapes and colors. Expressionists explored the individual's feelings about the subject. Sculptors expressed similar subjectivity in works that were increasingly popular in the renewal of urban spaces.

5. Functional Architecture. While much architecture in the late nineteenth century adhered to old styles, a new style was introduced that would ultimately revolutionize the look of cities. Functional architects stated that buildings should look like the purpose for which they are designed. Thus,

skyscrapers were built that looked like the steel, concrete and glass structures that they were.

6.   Music Old and New. Romantic and classical music continued into the late nineteenth century. However, there were some innovations in music that showed the influence of the revolutions in other artistic forms.

STUDY QUESTIONS

1.   With a newly literate public, newspapers became more popular. Who were the people instrumental in developing a popular press, and what was the philosophy behind their publications? Was the press free and objective? Is it now?

2.   What other forms of popular entertainment were developed to cater to the newly educated audience?

3.   How did some thinkers link military victories to racism? How did they define the idea of "race"? How do we define "race"? With what "race" did the Germans identify themselves?

4.   Some philosophers did not share an optimism that progress would inevitably make everything better. Discuss their views and tell what they believed was necessary to improve society.

5.   Describe some of the writers of realistic literature. How were the themes they explored related to the problems of the industrial age and the findings of the new scientists?

6.   Two new styles of painting that appeared as a reaction to traditional styles were impressionism and expressionism. What was each trying to achieve? Who were some major painters of each? What musicians are identified with each of these styles?

7.   Who were two of the famous sculptors of the late nineteenth century? How were their successes related to the growth of urbanization?

8.   In pragmatism, James said that if something works it is true. How is that principle consistent with functional architecture? What did architects mean by "form follows function"?

IDENTIFICATION

TRY TO USE EACH OF THESE TERMS AT LEAST ONCE IN ANSWERING
THE STUDY QUESTIONS

Joseph Pulitzer	W.R. Hearst	London *Times*
G.W. Hegel	Rudyard Kipling	Aryan
anti-Semitism	R. Wagner	F. Nietzsche
William James	pragmatism	Gustave Flaubert
Charles Dickens	George Eliot	Thomas Hardy
George Bernard	S. Turgenev	H. Ibsen
Shaw	impressionism	E. Manet
C. Monet	A. Renoir	P. Cézanne
V. van Gogh	expressionism	P. Picasso
C. Meunier	A. Rodin	L.H. Sullivan
C. Debussy	Igor Stravinsky	P. Tchaikovsky
Richard Strauss		

SAMPLE QUESTIONS

1.   Why did governments increasingly want to support public education? (p. 596)

2.   What countries eliminated illiteracy more quickly than the United States did? (p. 596)

3.   Beyond the core curriculum in education, what differing skills were taught boys and girls? (p. 596)

4.   Where did popular newspapers make their money? (p. 597)

5.   What did Nietzsche mean by the phrase "The will to power"? (p. 598)

6.   In what literary genres did realistic writers usually express themselves? (p. 599)

7.   What British author is known for his graphic detailing of the life of urban working class in industrial Britain? (p. 599)

8.   What did Ibsen criticize in his play, *A Doll's House*? (p. 600)

9.   How did scientific discoveries influence impressionist painting? (p. 600)

10.   Expressionist painters freely distorted images of nature in order to achieve what goal? (p. 601)

11.   What sculptor was the first to recognize the importance of the industrial proletariat and portray them in realistic statues? (p. 602)

12.   Give two examples of composers who expressed nationalism in their compositions. (p. 603)

REVIEW AND ANTICIPATION

1.   Review Darwin's ideas of survival of the fittest. How might those ideas on biology be misapplied to society by nineteenth-century racists?

2.   Review the challenge to Christianity discussed in the previous chapter. How do the ideas of the philosophers Nietzsche and William James continue the attack on Christian belief?

3.   Review the characteristics of romanticism. How do the realistic authors contrast with the romantics? How did the architects of romanticism contrast with the new functional architects?

Chapter 48
Politics, Democracy, and Nationalism,
1871-1914

OVERVIEW

Two themes dominated political life in Europe in the late nineteenth century: democracy and nationalism. The first was predominant in the west, leading to increasingly liberal governments. The second dominated the east, allowing more autocratic and unstable regimes to rule.

1. <u>Western Europe: The Spread and Reform of Democratic Institutions.</u> Although to varying degrees, all the western countries made progress toward increasing democratic participation in government and in legislating reform measures designed to alleviate the worst ills associated with industrialization. Great Britain was most advanced with reform bills that granted virtual full male suffrage and legislation that offered sickness, unemployment and other insurance. In addition, they took steps to reduce the power of the rich by steeply graduated income taxes and other similar legislation. In France the progress of democracy was made more difficult by the competing interests of various groups and by the striking political difference between radical Paris and the more conservative countryside. Nevertheless, democratic reforms were passed, increasing suffrage and giving some benefits to working people. Democratic reforms progressed in Italy and the northern European countries as suffrage was given to more men to include them in the political process. Along with these moves to democracy, nationalism grew bringing anti-Semitism and imperial arrogance to the fore.

2. <u>Eastern Europe: Conservatism, Militarism, and Nationalism.</u> While western Europe moved toward democratization and liberalism that encouraged individual freedom, people in eastern Europe focused on militant nationalism. The German Empire under skilled leadership prospered economically, surpassing other European states in industrial development. It built a strong military, and used nationalist sentiment to distract people from demanding too many liberal reforms. Russia was even more autocratic. Tsars agreed to make some concessions (like freeing the serfs), but for the most part such reforms came grudgingly and slowly. An opposition of radical socialists began to form. In southeast Europe, the lands of the Austrian and Ottoman empires, the main issue was nationalism. Language groups wanted to be able to express their national identity, causing potentially explosive instability in that region. Finally, this increased national sentiment was expressed in anti-Semitism and persecution of Jews throughout Europe.

Persecution was especially prevalent in the east and led to emigration and a growth of Zionism, the desire for a Jewish homeland.

MAP EXERCISE

1.   How many ethnic groups are located in the Austrian Empire?

2.   Which sections of this heterogeneous empire might be the least stable? Do you think the complexities of governing such a diverse area might increase the probability of autocratic government?

STUDY QUESTIONS

1.   Describe the process by which Britain moved to increased democracy in the late nineteenth century. What were the reforms? Who instituted them? Does our society still support these reform measures?

2.   Democratic government did not work as smoothly in France as in Great Britain. Why not? (Be sure to discuss the radical movements in Paris as part of your response.)

3.   Italy and the northern countries of western Europe also took steps to forward democracy. What were they?

4.   The growth of nationalism was a strong theme throughout Europe. Describe how this strong nationalism was expressed in each of the countries. Was aggressive nationalism stronger in eastern or western Europe? Why?

5.   While the German chancellor Bismarck had no particular sympathy for workers, he nevertheless passed legislation designed to help the working class. Why? What legislation did he pass?

6.   Contrast the foreign policy of Chancellor Bismarck with that of Wilhelm II. Which do you think would have worked more effectively in keeping Germany out of war?

7.   Describe the economic advances that took place in Germany in the late nineteenth century. Do any of the advantages Germany had then still serve to make Germany an economic leader?

8.   Tsar Alexander III attempted to suppress all types of reform. Why? Describe the Social Democratic party that arose in response. What forms of national rebellion against autocracy took place under the reign of Nicholas II?

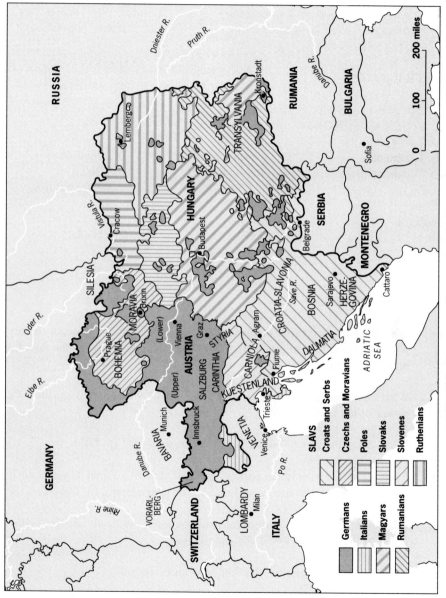

MAP 48.1 Language Groups, Austria-Hungary

215

9.   In Austria and the Ottoman Empire, the major political issue was not democratic reform. What was it? What kind of policy did Austria follow in trying to deal with this problem?

10.   After the 1880s there was an upsurge of anti-Semitism. Why? Where was it strongest? What were some responses on the part of Jewish populations?

IDENTIFICATION

TRY TO USE EACH OF THESE TERMS AT LEAST ONCE IN ANSWERING THE STUDY QUESTIONS

W.E. Gladstone	B. Disraeli	D. Lloyd George
Paris Commune	Alfred Dreyfus	von Bismarck
Wilhelm II	Triple Alliance	Three Emperor's
Alexander II	Alexander III	League
Nicholas II	"Red Sunday"	Duma
Lenin	Mensheviks	Bolsheviks
Zionism		

SAMPLE QUESTIONS

1.   Who were the two prime ministers in Britain in the mid-nineteenth century who sponsored reform bills that greatly increased the access to the vote for males? (p. 606)

2.   What legislative measures passed in Britain in 1909 specifically attacked the power of the rich? (p. 607)

3.   What group in France did the Dreyfus case discredit? (p. 608)

4.   France had many political parties, so what did the cabinet have to do in order to carry on the executive functions of government? (p. 608)

5.   What was the regional difference that weakened the newly unified Italian state? (p. 609)

6.   What country first granted the vote to women? (p. 609)

7.   Who was the chancellor of Germany for almost twenty years who shaped the development of that state? (p. 610)

8.   Why did the German chancellor persecute Socialists and Roman Catholics? (p. 610)

9.   What country did Wilhelm II offend when he pursued interests in the Balkans and the Ottoman Empire? (p. 611)

10.   Since Russia was not as industrialized as other countries in 1861, what was the most important reform introduced in that year by Alexander II? (p. 612)

11.   What group made up the leadership of the Social Democratic (Marxist) party in Russia? (p. 613)

12.   Who was the leader of the radical wing of the Social Democratic party in Russia (the Bolsheviks)? (p. 613)

13.   What contributed to a rise in anti-Semitism after the 1880s? (p. 615)

REVIEW AND ANTICIPATION

1.   Review the problems caused by industrialization and the solutions that had been posed by political thinkers from conservatives, liberals, and socialists. Which solutions seem to have been decided upon in western Europe? Which in eastern Europe?

2.   The growth of nationalism in Europe almost inevitably made each country more competitive with the other. Where do you think this competitiveness will be expressed next?

3.   Of all the regions/countries discussed in this chapter, which do you think is the most unstable and will cause problems in the succeeding decades? What region is the most unstable today? Why?

Chapter 49
Democracy, Expansion, Civil War, and Reform in the United States, 1800-1920

OVERVIEW

In the nineteenth century, the United States followed many of the same patterns that dominated in European society during the same time. Expansion, industrialization, and their accompanying problems shaped American society in the nineteenth century.

1.   Democracy and Geographic Expansion, 1800-1861. Democracy was forwarded in the United States with the presidencies of Jefferson and Jackson, both of whom extended the suffrage. Nationalism also grew during these years with the involvement in the War of 1812 and the acquisition of new territory that extended the lands of the United States to the Pacific Ocean. Population was increased by more immigration, especially from Europe. All this growth took place at the expense of the native Indian population.

2.   Slavery, Civil War, and Reconstruction, 1861-1877. Between 1861-1865, the United States was torn by civil war. The industrial, liberal North fought the agrarian, slave-holding, conservative South. The issue that focused much of the emotional energy between the two differing sides was that of slavery. The issue of slavery and its expansion to the new territories in the West had been brewing for some time, and the election of a Republican president committed to the restriction of slavery caused southern states to secede. The superior resources of the North ultimately won the prolonged war. Slavery was abolished and the union preserved.

3.   Industrialization and Urbanization, 1865-1901. After the Civil War, the United States joined other western nations as a leading industrial power. Industrialization proceeded in similar ways to that of European countries, but there were some elements that particularly characterized the American experience. Business and wealth became concentrated in the hands of a few individuals and corporations to a striking degree, and governmental policies favored these huge industrial firms. Another contrast in the American experience was that the United States government was behind in its willingness to address the social abuses of industrialization, and labor was unable to organize as early as in Europe. However, by the end of the nineteenth century, the United States had outstripped the world in industrial production.

4.   <u>Reform and Progressivism, 1901-1920.</u> From 1901 to 1920, the government finally took action to curb some of the excesses of the industrial boom of the previous half century. During this progressive era, large industrial trusts were limited, and laws passed to protect public health, welfare, and resources. By the end of this period, the United States had entered World War I and had fully joined the worldwide economic and political system.

STUDY QUESTIONS

1.   Describe the progress toward increased democratization that took place in the United States under Jefferson and Jackson. Contrast these developments with the political philosophy of the Founding Fathers and the Federalists.

2.   Describe the process by which the United States extended its borders to the Pacific Ocean. At the expense of what countries and what peoples did this expansion take place? Contrast the reality of the expansion with the idealized myth shown in the painting, *Manifest Destiny*, in Figure 49.1.

3.   Describe the progress of slavery in America from its inception to its abolition after the Civil War. What made slavery so entrenched in the South and not in the North?

4.   Contrast southern society and values with those in the North. Include in your discussion an analysis of Figures 49.2 and 49.3 and what they can show about the contrast between the two regions. What were the military advantages of each side?

5.   Compare and contrast the progress of industrialization in the United States with that in western Europe. (Be sure to include in your discussion a consideration of the plight of workers.) What differences that were established in the nineteenth century still persist today?

6.   What reforms were passed during the progressive era that addressed some of the excesses of the early years of American industrialization? What presidents sponsored these reforms?

IDENTIFICATION

TRY TO USE EACH OF THESE TERMS AT LEAST ONCE IN ANSWERING THE STUDY QUESTIONS

*Thomas Jefferson	Andrew Carnegie	*T. Roosevelt
War of 1812	J.P. Morgan	*W. Wilson

Federalists   *Andrew Jackson   Antitrust Acts
*A. Lincoln   Republican Party   American Federation
J.D. Rockefeller   C. Vanderbilt   of Labor
Samuel Gompers

CHRONOLOGY

List in chronological order the words in the Identification section that have an asterisk (*). As you list these items, put a circle around those that are contemporary.

SAMPLE QUESTIONS

1.   What gave a boost to feelings of American nationalism? (p. 618)

2.   From what countries did America get the land that extended its territories to the Pacific ocean? (Map 49.1)

3.   After 1840 from what countries did most of the immigrant groups come to the United States? (p. 619)

4.   What president marked the rise of a "common man" to the presidency and brought with that rise an attendant increase in suffrage? (p. 618)

5.   What invention made slavery very profitable? (p. 621)

6.   What political party was founded committed to the restriction of slavery? (p. 622)

7.   When were federal troops finally withdrawn from the South? (p. 622)

8.   When did the United States join other western nations as a leading industrial power? (p. 622)

9.   Who organized the first successful national labor organization in America? (p. 623)

10.   The American government favored one particular interest more than European nations did. What interest was this? (p. 623)

11.   What president began the progressive era's restrictions on large corporations? (p. 624)

12.   When did women get the vote in the United States? (p. 624)

REVIEW AND ANTICIPATION

1.   Review the principles upon which the United States was founded. Do you see the direction taken by the growing industrialization of the United States as consistent or inconsistent with those early principles?

2.   With the United States becoming a leading industrial power in the late nineteenth century, do you think it will be able to stay isolated from European politics and war?

Chapter 50
Imperialism

OVERVIEW

Between 1880 and 1914, the European powers embarked on new expansion around the world to build empires. Western powers struggled for control over territories in Asia, Africa, and the Pacific. The ensuing conquests irrevocably changed existing cultures and created problems that continue unresolved.

1. Causes of the New Imperialism. The search for empires surged in the late nineteenth century for a number of reasons. Industrial powers were looking for raw materials and markets for their production; nationalism and competition between the western powers spurred nations to conquer other peoples; and Christian missionaries were looking for new converts. The advanced science and technology of the West made control of nonindustrialized lands easier.

2. The Exploitation and Awakening of China. Until the nineteenth century, the old, self-sufficient society of China was able to keep itself isolated from western involvement. After that, however, the Manchu dynasty had weakened and western powers were able to force their way into China, insisting on trading monopolies and direct control over certain lands. The Chinese responded by an ineffective rebellion against western influence, and by an attempt to reform and modernize China itself.

3. The Emergence of Japan. At first Japan, like China, wanted to exclude western powers from its lands. Once its ports were forced open, however, the Japanese learned from the successes of the West and reorganized their society somewhat along western lines. They were successful and quickly created an industrial, militarized state that was able to enter the race for empires, beat Russia in a war, and take over parts of China.

4. Competition for the Strategic Near and Middle East. The Near and Middle East were important for their strategic location in the valuable trade with the Far East. Britain gained control of the important Suez Canal, but Germany and Russia engaged in political power struggles to also control parts of this valuable crossroad. By 1914, this region continued to be a site of contention.

5. The Scramble for Africa. After 1880, European powers raced to carve up Africa as part of their empires. They accomplished this without concern for the local populations. The Europeans clashed with each other in their

competition for empire, fighting the Boer War in South Africa, and engaging in power struggles in Morocco.

6.   The British Empire. The British Empire was the largest in the world, and it brought much prosperity to Britain. Britain governed its English-speaking colonies generously, granting them virtual independence under the status of dominion. Other colonies, like India, received some benefits from technical and medical improvements, but received no concessions toward self-governing.

7.   The Legacy of Imperialism. Western powers created empires with no consideration or even much awareness of their impact on lives, cultures, economies, or the environment of the countries they conquered. By the twentieth century, however, these issues could be ignored no longer.

MAP EXERCISE

See map on p. 224.

1.   On the map of Asia, locate the following countries: India, Russian Empire, Tibet, China, Manchuria, Japanese Empire, Korea, French Indochina, Dutch East Indies.

2.   On the map of Asia, locate the following cities: St. Petersburg, Moscow, Constantinople, Jerusalem, Bombay, Calcutta, Hanoi, Saigon, Beijing, Hong Kong, Tokyo.

3.   What areas on the borders of China were taken over by other powers? Why was Hong Kong important to the British? What long-term effect did the French takeover of Indochina have?

4.   What region do we usually refer to as the "Near East" and what region as the "Middle East"? Where is the Suez Canal? What bodies of water does it join? Why is it important?

See map on p. 225.

5.   On the map of Africa, which European countries held the most area? Which held the most prosperous areas (for trade? for raw materials)?

6.   Where is the Union of South Africa? Why is it called "Union" (that is, what is it a union of)? Why is Cape Town strategically important?

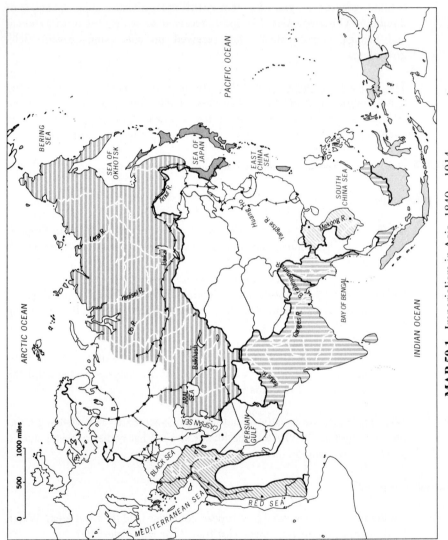

MAP 50.1 Imperialism in Asia, 1840 – 1914

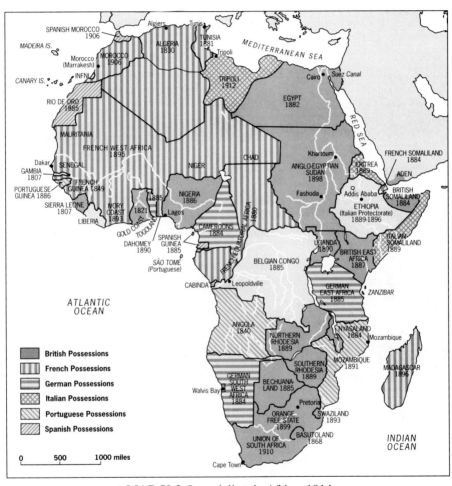

MAP 50.2 Imperialism in Africa, 1914

Legend:
- **British Possessions**
- **French Possessions**
- **German Possessions**
- **Italian Possessions**
- **Portuguese Possessions**
- **Spanish Possessions**

0   500   1000 miles

SPANISH MOROCCO 1906
MADEIRA IS.
Algiers   Tunis
MOROCCO 1906
Morocco (Marrakesh)
TUNISIA 1881
ALGERIA 1830
Tripoli
MEDITERRANEAN SEA
CANARY IS.
INFNI
RIO DE ORO 1885
TRIPOLI 1912
Cairo   Suez Canal
EGYPT 1882
RED SEA
MAURITANIA
FRENCH WEST AFRICA 1895
CHAD
Khartoum
FRENCH SOMALILAND 1884
ADEN
Dakar
GAMBIA 1807
SENEGAL
NIGER
ANGLO-EGYPTIAN SUDAN 1898
ERITREA 1889
BRITISH SOMALILAND 1884
FRENCH GUINEA 1849
PORTUGUESE GUINEA 1886
SIERRA LEONE 1807
IVORY COAST 1893
LIBERIA
GOLD COAST 1821
TOGOLAND
1885
NIGERIA 1886
Lagos
Fashoda
Addis Ababa
ETHIOPIA (Italian Protectorate) 1889-1896
ITALIAN SOMALILAND 1889
DAHOMEY 1890
SPANISH GUINEA 1885
CAMEROONS 1884
FRENCH EQUATORIAL AFRICA 1890
UGANDA 1890
BRITISH EAST AFRICA 1887
SÃO TOMÉ (Portuguese)
CABINDA
BELGIAN CONGO 1885
Leopoldville
GERMAN EAST AFRICA 1885
ZANZIBAR
ATLANTIC OCEAN
ANGOLA 1840
NORTHERN RHODESIA 1889
NYASALAND 1884
Mozambique
MOZAMBIQUE 1891
MADAGASCAR 1896
SOUTHERN RHODESIA 1889
GERMAN SOUTH WEST AFRICA 1884
Walvis Bay
BECHUANALAND 1885
Pretoria
SWAZILAND 1893
ORANGE FREE STATE 1899
BASUTOLAND 1868
UNION OF SOUTH AFRICA 1910
INDIAN OCEAN
Cape Town

STUDY QUESTIONS

1.   Discuss the causes for the growth of imperialism in the late nineteenth century. Which do you think is the most important? Why?

2.   How did the western powers force open China for trade? Which powers were the most successful?

3.   How did the Chinese respond to the western impositions? What reforms did they attempt? How successful were they?

4.   Contrast Japan's and China's response to contact with the West. What examples demonstrate Japan's successful entry into the military industrial world of the late nineteenth century?

5.   What powers struggled to exert control over the Near and Middle East? Why were these regions considered important? What role did the Ottoman Empire play in the scramble for influence in this region?

6.   Who fought in the Boer War? Where was this located? What were the issues and the outcome? Do you think the vigorous defense of land during the Boer War sheds light on that country's current struggles?

7.   What struggles between European powers took place over lands in Africa? Do you expect this to foreshadow a larger war?

8.   Contrast Britain's treatment of its English-speaking colonies with its other colonies (like India). What was the most effective way to govern? Why do you think Britain didn't treat them all the same?

9.   What impact did imperialism have on the conquered territories and peoples?

IDENTIFICATION

TRY TO USE EACH OF THESE TERMS AT LEAST ONCE IN ANSWERING THE STUDY QUESTIONS AND MAP EXERCISES

Treaty of Nanking	Boxer Rebellion	Manchu dynasty
Sun Yat-sen	Yuan	Matthew C. Perry
Suez Canal	Wilhelm II	Boer War
General Botha	dominion	East India Company

SAMPLE QUESTIONS

1.   What is a specific economic benefit to a country to create an empire? (p. 627)

2.   What political advantage would a country have by holding portions of the world as colonies? (p. 627)

3.   The British went to war with China in order to preserve their shipment of what commodity? (p. 629)

4.   What territory did the French take from China? (p. 629)

5.   What were the goals of the revolutionaries in the Boxer Rebellion? (pp. 629-630)

6.   What were the goals of Sun Yat-sen's party? (p. 630)

7.   Who forced open the ports of Japan to trade with the West? (p. 630)

8.   What did the Japanese borrow from the West as they reorganized their society? (p. 630)

9.   Before the development of oil resources after World War I, of what importance was the Middle East to western powers? (p. 631)

10.   Who controlled the Suez Canal after 1875? (p. 631)

11.   By 1914, which were the only two independent areas left in Africa? (p. 632)

12.   By 1914, what colonies were granted dominion status by Great Britain? (p. 635)

13.   Until 1858, who governed India? (p. 635)

REVIEW AND ANTICIPATION

1.   Review the growth of nationalism in Chapter 48. How was the struggle for overseas empires a logical extension of the struggles for power on the European continent? Review the nationalist feelings praised in romanticism in Chapter 41. How were the same sentiments described in the romantic authors expressed in the politics of imperialism?

2.   In the "Retrospect," you reviewed the dramatic changes that revolutionized western society between about 1776 and 1850. What were these revolutions, and which do you think had the most long-term impact on our society?

3.   In the "Retrospect," you also reviewed the dominance of nationalism and industrialization during the late nineteenth century. Consider how these two themes influenced the imperialism discussed in this chapter.

4.   Do you think the struggles between the European powers for empire will continue to be restricted to skirmishes outside Europe? Will the powers need to test their strength directly on each other?

5.   Which of the many colonies do you think will become trouble spots in the future?

Chapter 51
World War I, 1914-1918

OVERVIEW

The twentieth century opened with a crisis that was to shake the complacency of the nineteenth-century world and transform European society. This was a war of such intensity, that it left no one unaffected.

1. Origins of the War. Some of the origins of World War I lay in the long-developing tensions of the nineteenth century. Nationalism, militarism, and imperial and economic rivalries had been fermenting to an explosive level for some time. The detonator for this situation occurred in the Balkans, where Serbian nationalism confronted Austro-Hungarian interests. The alliances linking the European powers brought the major countries into this dispute, setting off a world war.

2. The Western Front. All sides expected the war to be won quickly and easily, but everyone misjudged the nature of modern warfare. After the initial German invasion of France stalled, the western front settled into a long, bloody stalemate along a long front of fortified trenches. New technology was developed that changed the nature of warfare and increased its human cost.

3. The Eastern Front. The war on the eastern front remained more mobile than the west, but the losses were equally high. Russia took immense losses as it tried to hold out against the better-prepared Germans. The war also was fought in the south and east, with Allied and Arab forces having successes against the Ottoman Empire.

4. The Home Front. This war required a total effort of society, and called for changes at home to support the war effort. Governments increasingly took control of their economies, retreating from the free market ideal; class and gender distinctions blurred as people were needed for a work force depleted of young men. Democratic processes were often ignored in the name of efficiency. The war was one that engaged civilian as well as military populations.

5. The Entry of the United States and the Victory of the Allies. Although ostensibly neutral at the beginning of the war, the United States favored the Allies. When the Germans began to attack American supply ships, the United States declared war. American supplies and men served to break the stalemate and secure an Allied victory. The government of Germany fell, and a civilian government signed a peace treaty.

6.   <u>The Peace Settlement.</u> The main powers at the peace conference were plagued with differing ideas. France wanted Germany weakened and the United States and Britain wanted a balance of power. Compromises were made that ultimately left all parties dissatisfied. Austria-Hungary and the Ottoman Empire were dissolved, leaving ethnic minorities with their own states. The League of Nations was formed to attempt to keep peace, although without the participation of the United States.

7.   <u>The Effects of World War I and the Peace Settlement.</u> The financial, material, and human losses of the war were immense and served to transform European society. The Treaty of Versailles left most parties dissatisfied and left a heritage of anger that would fester until war broke out again two decades later.

MAP EXERCISE

1.   Write in the names of the following countries: Spain, France, Great Britain, Belgium, Netherlands, Austria, Germany, Poland, Czechoslovakia, Yugoslavia, Rumania, Bulgaria, Serbia, Finland, Estonia, Latvia.

2.   What countries border Germany that might have German-speaking people?

3.   What countries border Serbia that would be threatened by instability in Serbia?

4.   What areas were lost by the old Russian Empire (later the Soviet Union)? Do you think it will be resentful of all that lost territory?

STUDY QUESTIONS

1.   What were the long-term causes of World War I? What was the precipitating incident?

2.   How have historians disputed the causes for World War I? What are the various positions on the causes? What do you think is the most important cause? Do you think this war could have been avoided?

3.   What was the German war plan? What caused it to fail? What finally was decisive in the Allied victory?

4.   Describe the nature of the new warfare. What new technologies were developed that changed the nature of war? Which of these innovations do you think will have the longest-term impact?

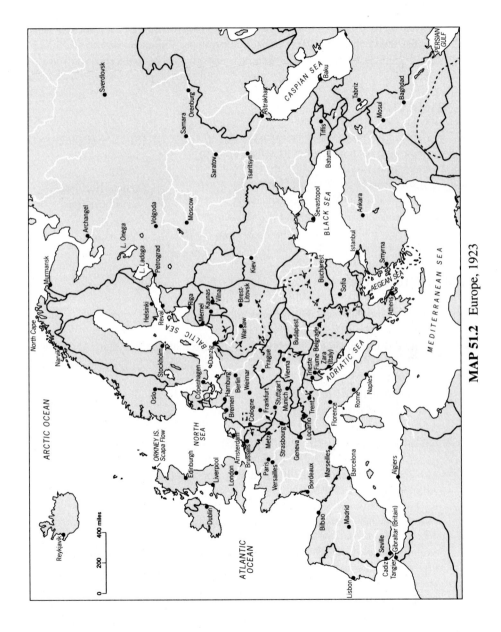

MAP 51.2 Europe, 1923

231

5.   In what ways did the civilian populations at home find their lives changed because of the war effort? How were the economic and political processes changed?

6.   What were the conflicting issues at the peace conference to end the war? What did each party want? What compromises did each have to make? Do you think the treaty was sufficiently just to resolve the issues and ensure peace?

IDENTIFICATION

TRY TO USE EACH OF THESE TERMS AT LEAST ONCE IN ANSWERING THE STUDY QUESTIONS AND MAP EXERCISES

Triple Alliance	Triple Entente	Francis Ferdinand
Central Powers	Schlieffen plan	war of attrition

Treaty of Brest-
  Litovsk
	Woodrow Wilson
	League of Nations
		Treaty of
		  Versailles

SAMPLE QUESTIONS

1.   What event triggered the outbreak of World War I? (p. 645)

2.   How did Germany get involved in a dispute that was between Austria and Serbia? (p. 645)

3.   Why did Italy not honor the alliance that would have drawn it into war on the side of Germany? (p. 645)

4.   What was the Schlieffen plan? (p. 645)

5.   In trench warfare, which is more important, offensive or defensive strategies? (p. 647)

6.   What did the Treaty of Brest-Litovsk accomplish? (p. 647)

7.   Why did governments retreat from free market economics during the war? (p. 648)

8.   What provided the immediate impetus for the entry of the United States into the war? (p. 649)

9. What new weapon developed by the British proved to be decisive in breaking through the German lines on the western front? (p. 649)

10. From what countries were the "Big Four," the most important negotiators at the peace conference? (Figure 51.3)

11. What did the peace treaty decide to do about the ethnic minorities in the Austro-Hungarian Empire? (p. 652)

12. Why wasn't the League of Nations effective? (pp. 652-653)

REVIEW AND ANTICIPATION

1. What old animosities between the European states were played out in this war?

2. The new states formed in the Balkans were supposed to reflect the desires for national identity there. Was that successful? Will that area continue to be unstable?

3. If you were a general who had just come through this war, how do you think you would plan for the next one? What would you fortify?

Chapter 52
Revolution and Communism in Russia

OVERVIEW

The pressures of war overwhelmed the ineffective tsarist government and it was swept from power by a revolution that brought a kind of communist government to the country. That government became a threatening totalitarian regime that formed a haunting specter to the West into the late twentieth century.

1. The Russian Revolution of 1917. Tsar Nicholas II had continued the Russian policies of conservative resistance to change in spite of pressure for reform. Dissatisfaction increased as the war exerted growing pressure on the economy. Finally, in 1917 bread riots and strikes in Petrograd forced the resignation of Nicholas II. A Provisional Government enacted many liberal reforms, but its continued participation in the unpopular war allowed more radical elements to exert their influence.

2. The Rise of the Bolsheviks. The instability caused by the continuing war allowed Bolsheviks (the radical wing of the Social Democratic party in exile) to come back to Russia. Lenin, the Bolshevik leader, advocated a program that would bring workers and peasants together to build a socialist society that would be led by an elite group of party members. Lenin further promised to end the war. With this program, the Bolsheviks led a second revolution that brought down the government.

3. The Bolsheviks in Power, 1917-1927. Upon taking power, Lenin instituted a number of measures to begin to bring socialism to the new U.S.S.R. In addition, he negotiated the devastating treaty to end the war against Germany. The new regime was further weakened by a civil war in which the "Whites" supported by the West fought the "Reds," supporters of the Bolshevik revolution. The Reds won, but at great cost. Lenin introduced the NEP, a compromise with capitalism, to try to restore the economy. It was beginning to succeed, but Lenin then died. Leadership passed to Joseph Stalin, who introduced a new initiative to advance socialism in the U.S.S.R.

4. The Five-Year Plans and the Purges. Stalin attempted to transform the economy and society of the U.S.S.R. into an industrial communist society. He established five-year plans during which society would be marshaled to accomplish certain planned goals. They included collectivizing agriculture at a cost of much human suffering. To enforce his policies, Stalin "purged" the party and the country of dissenters. By the end of the 1930s, the U.S.S.R. had been converted into a significant industrial power.

5.   Totalitarian Control. Under the totalitarian regime that Lenin's and Stalin's highly hierarchic order introduced, society was transformed. Individual freedoms were curtailed, but education was fostered in a land that had long neglected it. The arts were also encouraged, but censorship made sure the art was not objectionable to the regime. Women were given equal access to the workplace, but continued to have full responsibilities for care of the home. Religion was banned and church property appropriated.

6.   The Soviet Union and the World. For the most part, mutual suspicion governed the relationship between the U.S.S.R. and the West. The Soviets fostered Communist parties in other countries, and western countries refused to recognize the new Soviet government for quite some time. The animosities were temporarily suspended when the western powers and the U.S.S.R. needed each other to counter the threat of fascism.

STUDY QUESTIONS

1.   What pressures led to the Revolution of 1917? What reforms did the resulting Provisional Government plan to implement? What caused the failure of the Provisional Government?

2.   How did the Bolsheviks come to power? Who were their leaders, and what was their program? Include a description of the civil war in your analysis.

3.   What pressures caused Lenin to try a "New Economic Policy"? What was this program?

4.   What was the difference in socialist philosophy between Stalin and Trotsky? Who prevailed to become the head of the party?

5.   What were the objectives of the Five-Year Plans? How successful were they? What relationship was there between this attempt to quickly and radically transform society and Stalin's use of purges to eliminate dissent?

6.   How were the collective state farms run during Stalin's era? What were the advantages and disadvantages of this form of agriculture?

7.   What was the political organization of the Soviet Union? How is this consistent with Lenin's vision of the way the state should be organized?

8.   Describe the changes brought about in Soviet society by the Communists. What was their position on education and the arts? What role were women to have in the new society? To what degree did women achieve equality?

9.   Describe the changing relationship between the U.S.S.R. and the western powers from 1917 through 1933. What increased the animosity between the two sides? What caused them to work together for a while? What can we learn from this about foreign relations?

IDENTIFICATION

TRY TO USE EACH OF THESE TERMS AT LEAST ONCE IN ANSWERING THE STUDY QUESTIONS

*Nicholas II	Rasputin	*Provisional
soviet	*A. Kerensky	Government
Duma	*Lenin	Bolsheviks
Mensheviks	*Leon Trotsky	*NEP
*Treaty of Brest-	*Joseph Stalin	*kulaks*
Litovsk	*Five-Year Plans	Comintern
*Great Purges	politburo	

CHRONOLOGY

List in chronological order the words in the Identification section that have an asterisk (*). As you list these items, put a circle around those that are contemporary.

SAMPLE QUESTIONS

1.   What was the soviet? (p. 656)

2.   What caused the failure of the Provisional Government? (pp. 656-657)

3.   Who was the leader of the Bolshevik wing of the Social Democratic party who had been in exile until 1917? (p. 657)

4.   What issue more than any other caused the Kerensky government to fail and brought the Bolsheviks to power? (p. 657)

5.   Under whose leadership did Lenin place all industry and commerce? (p. 658)

6.   What industries were allowed to operate under private ownership under the NEP? (p. 658)

7.   Who became leader of the U.S.S.R. after the death of Lenin? (p. 658)

8.   What did Stalin mean by the phrase, "socialism in one country"? (p. 659)

9.   What are "five-year plans"? (p. 660)

10.   In what industries were the five-year plans most successful? (p. 661)

11.   In the Soviet political system, what office was the most powerful in the government? (p. 662)

12.   What was the Soviet policy toward organized religion? (p. 664)

13.   What was the Comintern organized for? (p. 664)

REVIEW AND ANTICIPATION

1.   Review the main ideas of Karl Marx. How did Lenin modify these ideas to make them applicable in the agrarian country of Russia?

2.   Review the ideals and practices of the Reign of Terror in the French Revolution. Do you see any parallels between that and Stalin's Great Purges?

3.   What elements of the Soviet regime do you think the West is going to find most threatening in the long run?

Chapter 53
The Rise of Fascism and Authoritarianism

OVERVIEW

Victory in World War I was supposed to make the world safe for democracy. Instead, economic pressures and fears of communism led to a rise in militant nationalism that created totalitarian regimes and threatened world peace.

1.   Totalitarianism, Fascism, and Authoritarianism. In the 1920s and 1930s, there was a growth of political systems that departed from and threatened the liberal democracies that had been gaining strength in the nineteenth century. Totalitarian regimes suppressed individual rights in favor of an ideology controlled by the government. Some were totalitarianism of the Left (communism), and some were totalitarianism of the Right (fascism). Right-wing authoritarian regimes were conservative attempts to preserve the status quo by exertion of power, but were less ideologically based than fascism.

2.   Mussolini Creates the First Fascist State. Italy emerged from World War I with a battered economy and battered national pride. The government was unable to deal with the economic crisis and the threat of Marxism. Mussolini organized unemployed veterans into terror squads and forced his way into office. He soon became a dictator and suppressed opposition. He reorganized the economy to benefit capitalists and he began to rebuild the military to recapture national greatness.

3.   The Weimar Republic in Germany. The new republic set up after the fall of the empire after World War I was established as a liberal democracy. However, the republic was troubled with severe economic problems and animosity left from the severe terms of the peace treaty. In spite of some progress made by the government, power was moving to extremist political parties.

4.   The Rise of Hitler and National Socialism. Hitler used his gifts of charismatic oratory and leadership to attract those disenchanted with the Weimar Republic. He organized a political party, the National Socialist (Nazi), as the German fascist party. His program called for recognition of the Germans as the master "race," repudiation of the Treaty of Versailles, reconquest of lost territories, and persecution of the Jews. His domestic policy was less well developed, but it was designed to persecute Jews, destroy communism and labor unions, and build a strong, military state.

5.   The Triumph of Hitler. By 1932, Hitler's Nazi party had so many supporters that it got a plurality in the elections to the legislative body. The president,

Hindenburg, had no choice but to appoint Hitler as Chancellor of Germany. Shortly after he became chancellor, he took steps to destroy the opposition parties, and was awarded dictatorial powers.

6.   Nazi Germany. Once Hitler had taken power, he reorganized the state along the lines of his political philosophy. He removed individual freedoms, spurred the economy by rearmament, reshaped education and family life to suit Nazi purposes and began to persecute political opponents, homosexuals, gypsies and especially Jews.

7.   Authoritarian Regimes in Eastern and Southern Europe. Liberal democracies failed to take root in most of eastern Europe. Power was taken by either royal or military dictators, and these authoritarian regimes emphasized nationalism and militarism. They shared many of the same qualities as Fascists, but were not fully so. Portugal and Spain came under the rule of right-wing dictators during the 1930s.

8.   The Triumph of Authoritarianism in Japan. Three groups struggled for power in postwar Japan. Rich industrialists and the military aligned against those wanting liberal democracy. The military invaded Manchuria and stirred nationalist zeal. Democracy was crushed and the military took over and began imperial expansion in earnest.

STUDY QUESTIONS

1.   Contrast totalitarianism of the Right with that of the Left. What were the characteristics of Fascist ideology? How do right-wing authoritarian regimes differ from Fascist ones?

2.   What were the economic problems that troubled Italy after World War I? How did Mussolini reorganize the economy to address these problems? How well do you think his solution would work?

3.   How did Mussolini take power? How did Hitler take power? Compare and contrast the two.

4.   What problems plagued the Weimar Republic in Germany? How many of these problems were the result of the peace treaty?

5.   Describe the philosophy and political program of Germany's National Socialist party. How is it similar to Mussolini's fascism and how is it different?

6.   Historians disagree on the causes of nazism. What reasons are suggested? What do you think is the most plausible reason for the support given to Hitler?

7.   Hitler subordinated all activities of the German state to the purpose of making a military comeback. Describe how this was true in economics, education, and family life.

8.   Describe the nature of the authoritarian regimes in eastern Europe. Why do you think that region that was newly freed from Austria had so much trouble sustaining democratic institutions?

9.   How did the military class take control in Japan? Why did the powerful industrialists support them? In their hands, what were the key elements of Japanese policy during the 1930s (See Figure 53.4)?

IDENTIFICATION

TRY TO USE EACH OF THESE TERMS AT LEAST ONCE IN ANSWERING THE STUDY QUESTIONS

fascism	B. Mussolini	corporate state
Weimar Republic	National	Nazi
Hindenburg	Socialist	*Führer*
Gestapo	A. Hitler	Francisco Franco
zaibatsu	H. Himmler	

SAMPLE QUESTIONS

1.   What is the definition of a totalitarian system? (p. 667)

2.   Who first initiated fascism? (p. 667)

3.   What was Mussolini's relationship with the pope? (p. 669)

4.   What was Mussolini's policy toward labor unions? (p. 668)

5.   Why did French troops occupy the Ruhr Valley in Germany in 1923? (p. 670)

6.   What did Hitler mean by the "Aryan" race? (p. 670)

7.   How did Hitler come to be dictator of Germany? (p. 673)

8.   Why is the strong use of propaganda crucial for totalitarian dictatorships? (p. 674)

9.   According to the Nazis, what was the sole purpose of education? (p. 674)

10.   With what countries did Hitler make an alliance in 1937 that was to be an alliance for military expansion? (pp. 674-675)

11.   What solved the unemployment problem in Germany? (p. 674)

12.   What was the only eastern European country to maintain a parliamentary democracy until conquered by Hitler? (p. 675)

13.   What military venture made it easier for the military class in Japan to take power? (p. 676)

REVIEW AND ANTICIPATION

1.   Review the political philosophy of conservatism, particularly as articulated in the nineteenth century by Edmund Burke. This was the far right before the rise of fascism. How is fascism different from this position? Why is fascism considered to be on the right rather than the left?

2.   Some historians believe that Nazism was an aberration of history, to appear only at that time under those circumstances. Do you agree, or do you think the far right can appear at other times under other circumstances?

Chapter 54
Paralysis of the Democratic West

OVERVIEW

Victory in World War I did not guarantee that the western democratic powers would escape from the postwar problems. Economic depression and a crisis in values kept the democracies from responding early and effectively to the challenge of fascism.

1. <u>Challenges of the 1920s and 1930s.</u> The victorious democracies faced several serious challenges in the postwar years. They had to solve the problems of moving people and production from a wartime to a civilian economy; they had to respond to disillusionment with efforts to preserve peace; they had to confront severe economic depression, and respond to political extremism from the Left and Right.

2. <u>The Harassed British Empire.</u> The war weakened Britain's hold on its empire, and it was forced to grant freedom to dominions to keep their loyalty. At home, economic problems caused great distress, and political parties struggling between conservative and left-wing solutions were unable to solve the problems that plagued Britain.

3. <u>Frustrated France.</u> The war had been fought in large part on French soil, and the resulting devastation of life and property created severe hardships for the French economy. Conservative politicians remained in power in spite of the pressure from the Socialist Left that wanted social reforms. France was unable to confront effectively the challenge of the rising military powers.

4. <u>The United States and the Great Depression.</u> The United States emerged from the war in a strengthened economic and political position. It responded by retreating to isolationism and enjoying an unsound temporary prosperity during the 1920s. The stock market crash in 1929 brought the United States into a serious, long-lasting depression that affected most European countries. The Depression stimulated new economic policies involving more government intervention in the economy, but the Depression ultimately would end only with the renewal of wartime production.

5. <u>Disillusionment and Uncertainty in Thought and Culture.</u> The growing crises in the western democracies were expressed in cultural trends. Philosophers argued that the West was in decline; novelists wrote disturbing introspective fiction; art movements depicted purposelessness; and Freud's ideas emphasizing the irrational and unconscious were popularized.

6. The Road to War. By the 1930s the world was moving quickly to war. The League of Nations had proved ineffective in stopping aggression in Manchuria and Ethiopia. The western democracies stood by while Fascist generals overthrew the legitimate government of Spain, and they were unwilling to interfere when Hitler broke the terms of the Treaty of Versailles and invaded neighboring countries. Finally, the West could stand by no longer and when Hitler invaded Poland, Great Britain and France declared war.

STUDY QUESTIONS

1. What were the four general challenges that confronted the western democracies after the postwar era? Which of these challenges grew directly from the Treaty of Versailles, and which from the general experience of war? Which do you think will be the most threatening?

2. Describe the economic problems that plagued Britain after World War I. How did the political parties attempt to address these problems? Why were they unsuccessful?

3. How were the economic problems of France different from those of Great Britain? What political agenda did the Popular Front propose to resolve these problems? How many of these socialist reforms do we have in place today?

4. Describe the retreat of the United States into isolationism after World War I.

5. What triggered the Great Depression? What policies made it worse? What did the government do to try to recover?

6. All these problems generated feelings of despair and hopelessness. Describe some of the cultural movements and great thinkers/artists who expressed this despair.

7. What events demonstrated the ineffectiveness of the League of Nations? What made the League unable to stop aggression? How has the United Nations been able to avoid these problems?

8. What were the issues in the Spanish Civil War? What side represented the legitimate government? What side was supported by Germany and Italy? What kind of support was given by the western democracies? Who won?

9.   What was the progress of Hitler's aggression? What areas was Hitler able to take without opposition? Why? What finally galvanized the West to declare war?

10.   In spite of strong ideological differences between communism and fascism, what persuaded Stalin to sign an agreement with Hitler?

IDENTIFICATION

TRY TO USE EACH OF THESE TERMS AT LEAST ONCE IN ANSWERING THE STUDY QUESTIONS

*Locarno Era	Statute of Westminster	Ramsay MacDonald
Popular Front	*Great Depression	Léon Blum
Maginot line	isolationism	*Woodrow Wilson
*Warren G. Harding	O. Spengler	*Franklin D.
*New Deal	S. Freud	Roosevelt
Ortega y Gasset	Loyalists	F. Kafka
F. Franco		Munich Conference

CHRONOLOGY

List in chronological order the words in the Identification section that have an asterisk (*). As you list these items, put a circle around those that are contemporary.

SAMPLE QUESTIONS

1.   What efforts were made to reduce international tensions during the 1920s? (p. 679)

2.   How did the Great Depression in the United States affect the European economies? (p. 679)

3.   What did the Statute of Westminster do for Britain's dominions? (p. 680)

4.   How had France planned to pay off a staggering war debt? (p. 681)

5.   A coalition of what parties constituted France's "Popular Front"? (p. 681)

6.   What was the position of the United States on the League of Nations? (p. 682)

7.   Why were the Scandinavian democracies able to get through the Great Depression with relative ease? (p. 683)

8.   What governmental economic policies worsened the Depression? (p. 683)

9.   What finally brought the United States to full recovery from the Depression? (p. 684)

10.   What economic policies constituted the New Deal? (p. 683)

11.   What were philosophers like Spengler and Ortega y Gasset arguing? (p. 684)

12.   What country refused to comply with the League of Nations' attempt to withhold oil from Mussolini because of his invasion of Ethiopia, and thus doomed the sanctions? (p. 685)

13.   What countries was Hitler able to take without opposition? (p. 686)

14.   What triggered the European's declaration of war against Germany? (p. 688)

REVIEW AND ANTICIPATION

1.   Review the ideals of fascism as described in the previous chapter. Were the actions of Hitler described here surprising in the light of his stated aims? Should the western democracies have been less willing to appease him at the beginning?

2.   Review the ideals of liberalism that strongly emphasized individual freedoms. Is there anything implicit in these ideas that made it harder for the democracies to respond to the challenges of depression and fascism?

3.   Do you think the United States will be able to sustain its isolationist policy in the face of the threat of fascism? Will it try?

Chapter 55
World War II, 1939-1945

OVERVIEW

World War II was an even more devastating war than World War I. The loss of life and the destruction of property was astounding. Western society will be dramatically transformed by this catastrophe.

1. Two Years of Axis Triumph. The first two years of the war marked striking victories for the Axis powers. It looked as if the western democracies would be unable to withstand Hitler's advance. Continental Europe was under Hitler's control. The tide began to turn when Hitler was unable to defeat Britain by air attacks; Mussolini was unable to win in the Middle East; and the German armies were unable to defeat the Soviet Union before the winter set in. The stage was set for the West to begin to turn the tide.

2. The Nazi Empire. All the resources of Germany were not used in the war effort. Many were taken up in implementing Hitler's racial policy. Many people were taken to concentration camps and exterminated in an effort to eliminate groups, particularly Jews. Resistance movements established underground networks to try to undermine the German occupation.

3. The United States' Entry into the War. At first the United States preserved its isolationist policy in theory, but it did support Britain's resistance with aid. The United States entered the war formally against the Axis powers when Japan bombed the U.S. fleet at Pearl Harbor.

4. The Home Front. As in World War I, it was necessary to mobilize the whole society in support of such total wars. However, World War II introduced even more trials on the civilian population. Cities were the targets of bombing by both sides, and atomic bombs caused particular horror. Germany's racial policies fell harshly on civilians, and in the United States, Japanese-Americans were harshly treated. The lines between military and civilian were blurred during this war.

5. The Climax and Turning Point of the War, June - August 1942. In 1942, the allies with the help of the United States were able to stop the momentum of the Axis advance. The Soviets successfully halted the German advance in a fierce defense of Stalingrad, after which the Germans slowly retreated before Soviet advances. In Egypt, the German army was defeated by British and American forces, and in the Pacific the American navy won a decisive battle against the Japanese fleet which allowed American forces to slowly recapture the Pacific.

6.   Victory. The war came slowly but certainly to a conclusion on all fronts. With many casualties, the Russians pushed the Germans back and entered Berlin. On the western front, the Allies extensively bombed German cities and advanced through Sicily into Italy. The main invasion took place in 1944 with a landing in Normandy. The Allies then pushed the Germans back. On the Pacific front, Americans had been slowly retaking islands held by the Japanese. The Japanese surrendered after the United States dropped two atomic bombs on Japanese cities. The devastating war was over.

STUDY QUESTIONS

1.   What immediate military successes did the German armies have? What helped them gain such rapid victories?

2.   What countries was Hitler unable to conquer immediately? What prevented him? Why did he violate his pact with the U.S.S.R. and invade?

3.   Describe the racial policy known as Hitler's "New Order." What "races" were favored and which were persecuted? How does he use the word "race"? Do we define races as Hitler did?

4.   What did resistance movements do?

5.   Before the United States formally entered the war, what was its position? What support did it give Great Britain, and what was the philosophic position articulated by Roosevelt and Churchill?

6.   What brought the United States into the war? Why did Japan attack?

7.   How did the experience of civilians during World War I differ from that during World War II? What was the impact of new technology on civilian populations in warfare? Does this trend continue to be true today?

8.   What were the decisive turning points in the three theaters of the war? How were these turning points followed up leading to victory in each of the theaters? Which of these caused the most casualties?

IDENTIFICATION

TRY TO USE EACH OF THESE TERMS AT LEAST ONCE IN ANSWERING THE STUDY QUESTIONS

blitzkrieg	Charles de Gaulle	Winston Churchill
D. MacArthur	Axis powers	F.D. Roosevelt

Battle of   Pearl Harbor   Battle of Midway
  Britain   Atlantic Charter

SAMPLE QUESTIONS

1.   While Hitler invaded Poland, what territories did the Soviet Union annex?
      (p. 690)

2.   What kept Hitler from conquering Britain? (pp. 691-692)

3.   What groups of people did Hitler attempt to exterminate and about how
      many total people were killed in Nazi camps? (p. 693)

4.   What event precipitated the United States' formal entry into the war? (pp.
      694-695)

5.   What battle marked the turning point of the German advance in the
      U.S.S.R.? (pp. 695-696)

6.   What naval battle was decisive in stopping the momentum of the Japanese
      fleet? (p. 698)

7.   Where did the landing occur in which the Anglo-American forces crossed the
      Channel to open the western front? (p. 699)

8.   What happened to Hitler and Mussolini at the end of the war? (p. 700)

9.   What caused Japan to surrender? (p. 700)

REVIEW AND ANTICIPATION

1.   What military venture precipitated the destruction of Napoleon's empire? Is
      this similar to Hitler's mistake?

2.   How influential do you expect members of resistance movements to be after
      the overthrow of Hitler's occupation? Do you expect these people to support
      the political Left or Right?

3.   Of all the devastating things that were introduced during this war, what do
      you think will cause the most fear in the coming decades?

Chapter 56
The Recovery of Europe and the Superpowers, 1945-1980s

OVERVIEW

In 1945 Europe faced two huge problems: 1) How to rebuild the cities devastated by the war and care for the people cruelly dislocated; and 2) How to cope with the two superpowers who confronted each other in the Cold War. The first problem was resolved remarkably quickly; the second lasted for over forty years.

1.   The Settlement and the Cold War. Even before the war was over, the mutual suspicions that had existed between the Soviet Union and the West began to come to the fore. The Allies agreed to divide Germany and the Soviet Union insisted upon maintaining control over the recently liberated Eastern European countries. This suspicion introduced the Cold War, during which the U.S.S.R. attempted to be secure and spread communism, and the United States insisted upon containing Soviet influence and preventing the spread of communism. This long power struggle was expressed in many areas: Berlin, Cuba, Korea, Vietnam, etc. The two sides solidified their positions with a series of defensive alignments. There were times when the Cold War seemed to ease a bit, but in the 1980s it was clear that the two sides were still engaged in the struggle.

2.   Revival of a Divided Europe and the West. After the war as part of the reconstruction of Europe, the western powers returned to liberal democracy, heavily influenced by socialism, as a predominant form of government. The European countries also moved toward greater cooperation with each other in economic and military alliances. While there were many similar patterns among the western nations, there were nevertheless individual differences. Britain's economy and empire never fully recovered from the war and it continues to fight high unemployment. France had more resources to draw upon and developed central economic planning and social welfare programs and a strong economy. The real economic success was seen in the German Federal Republic which developed a remarkably strong economy and a solid democratic government. West Germany also took the lead in opening lines of communication with the Soviet Union and in turning environmental policy into a political party. Italy also built a republic out of the shambles of the fallen Fascist regime, but was always plagued by economic troubles that helped make the communist party a force. The countries of Southern Europe, Spain, Portugal, and Greece, shared a common political path -- they broke from authoritarian rule in the 1970s, established democratic forms of government and finally elected a Socialist government. The United States emerged from the war with an economic vigor that lasted for many years.

The United States was dominated by the Cold War and fear of communism and with the problem of integration of African-Americans into society. Politically the United States moved through social reform and conservative reaction as did the European countries, but never as far to the left.

3.   Integration and International Organizations. The experience of the war and the Cold War demonstrated that no country was strong enough to stand alone. Alliances were critical in the twentieth century. Some alliances (like NATO and the Warsaw Pact) were military, but others were economic. The latter, most particularly the European Economic Community, have been a striking success. The United Nations also has been able to make an impact on world peace.

MAP EXERCISE

1.   On the map of Europe, write in the names of the following countries: Norway, Sweden, Finland, Soviet Union, Poland, East Germany, West Germany, Czechoslovakia, Austria, Hungary, Rumania, Bulgaria, Yugoslavia, Italy, Switzerland, Belgium, Netherlands, France, Spain, Portugal, Great Britain, Ireland.

2.   Which countries were members of the Communist Block and which countries were in the NATO alliance?

3.   Which countries remained unaligned in 1950? Which countries do you think were most vulnerable to the tensions between the two sides? Is there any relationship between vulnerability and being unaligned?

4.   Which countries are members of the European Economic Community (the Common Market)?

5.   Which countries in Eastern Europe attempted to revolt against Soviet control?

STUDY QUESTIONS

1.   The mutual suspicions that led to the post-1945 Cold War had built for a long time. What events had contributed to these attitudes before World War II? What events during the war exacerbated these feelings even while the U.S.S.R. was allied with the West? What decisions made at conferences during the end of the war set the stage for continued animosity?

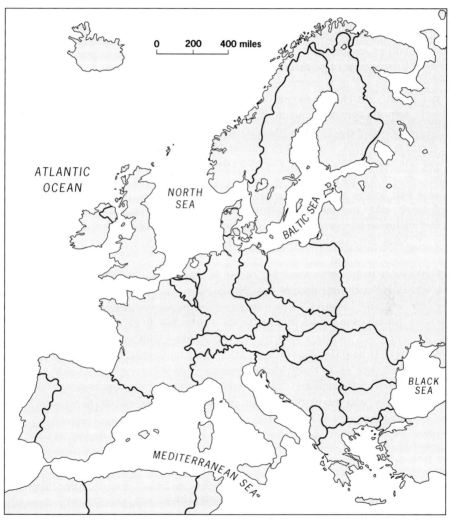

MAP 56.1 Europe During the Cold War

2.   What were the goals of the two sides in the Cold War? How did the great powers express these goals in political actions around the world? Consider Eastern Europe, Germany, Korea, and Cuba.

3.   Explain each of the following and tell how it fits the political expression of the Cold War: Truman Doctrine, Marshall Plan, NATO, Warsaw Pact.

4.   What does *détente* refer to? What were some examples of policies that would fall under this term? What events in the late 1970s and early 1980s demonstrated that détente was not a long-term state?

5.   One of the trends in Western Europe during the postwar years was a more central economic plan and a movement toward socialism (nationalization of industries and social welfare reforms, etc.). Describe these trends in each of the Western European countries, noting which political parties supported these reforms. During what years did there tend to be a conservative reaction against such reforms?

6.   To what degree did the United States enact similar social reforms? Under what administrations? When did the postwar prosperity end in the United States? When did the conservative reaction set in?

7.   What were some examples of social dissatisfaction that took place in the 1960s in Europe and the United States?

8.   Describe the model of government established in Eastern Europe after the war. How is this consistent with the Soviet Union's stated goals during the war? How did some countries try to gain more independence?

9.   Describe the military and nonmilitary organizations that have served to tie Europe and the world together. What are the goals of each? Which are the most successful? What are the drawbacks of each?

IDENTIFICATION

TRY TO USE EACH OF THESE TERMS AT LEAST ONCE IN ANSWERING THE STUDY QUESTIONS AND MAP EXERCISES

Cold War	C. de Gaulle	NATO
Marshall Plan	Fidel Castro	German Democratic
German Federal	*Brezhnev	Republic
Republic	European Economic	*Strategic Defense
*Korean War	Community	Initiative
Tito	*Yalta	M. Thatcher

*Khrushchev   Truman Doctrine   United Nations

Joseph McCarthy   Warsaw Pact   solidarity

stagflation   *Berlin Wall   Martin Luther King,

Lech Walesa   *Cuban Missile Crisis   Jr.

CHRONOLOGY

List in chronological order the words in the Identification section that have an asterisk (*). As you list these items, put a circle around those that are contemporary.

SAMPLE QUESTIONS

1.   What is the "Cold War"? (p. 703)

2.   Who attended the conference at Yalta to decide how to end the war? (Figure 56.2)

3.   What did the Allies decide to do with Germany after the victory? (p. 703)

4.   Who was to keep Eastern Europe in its sphere of influence? (p. 704)

5.   By 1950, what was the only Eastern European state that was not dominated by the Soviet Union? (p. 705)

6.   What are the German Democratic Republic and the German Federal Republic? (p. 706)

7.   What policies of the Reagan presidency heightened tensions between the United States and the U.S.S.R.? (p. 707)

8.   Who was the president of the Fifth French Republic that brought France into economic prosperity and concentrated on building French prestige abroad? (p. 710, Figure 56.3)

9.   What leader of the African-American movement was murdered in 1968? (p. 713)

10.   Who was the successor of Stalin who attempted to loosen the tight hold on Soviet society? (p. 714)

11.   In the late 1940s, governments and economies of Eastern Europe were established upon what model? (p. 715)

12.   What is the name of the workers' union in Poland that was influential in forcing the Communist government to grant concessions? (p. 717)

13.   What was the purpose of the European Economic Community? (p. 717)

14.   What at times has hampered the United Nations' ability to act? (p. 718)

REVIEW AND ANTICIPATION

1.   Review the devastation the U.S.S.R. experienced during World War I and the terms of the Treaty of Brest-Litovsk. To what degree do you think Soviet policy in Eastern Europe was influenced by those events?

2.   Review the importance of resistance movements during the war against fascism. To what degree do you think the movement of the European nations toward socialism was shaped by the left-wing resistance movements?

3.   Do you think Eastern Europe will be content to stay under Soviet domination? What country do you think will successfully rebel first?

Chapter 57
Society and Culture
in the Twentieth Century

OVERVIEW

Western society in the twentieth century has continued some of the trends of disillusionment and anxiety that became apparent after World War I. But it has added new productivity and experimentation which are signs of a vigorous society.

1. Western Society in the Twentieth Century. Since the postwar baby boom, birth rates have declined in much of the West. Population is more mobile, more urban, and focuses on education and technical expertise to enter the middle class in a postindustrial world. Families have grown smaller and, increasingly, both partners are in the work force. Women's movements have grown up to address inequalities that persist into the twentieth century. Government and educational institutions have had to absorb some of the responsibility for the social welfare of citizens. However, problems in society remain, such as drug abuse, poverty, crime, and disease.

2. Religion and Theology in the Twentieth Century. Christian churches have suffered a decline in the twentieth century. Efforts have been made to bring Christian churches together and to make traditional Christian religion meaningful to the modern world.

3. Twentieth-Century Science. Since World War II, science increasingly has been supported by government and business in an effort to link it with technology. In physics increasing progress has been made in probing the atom and exploring the universe. Biological sciences have made dramatic discoveries that have led to improved (and increasingly expensive) public health. All the social sciences have made strides forward, and all have taken advantage of the computer as the most significant tool of the late twentieth century.

4. Twentieth-Century Culture. Philosophy after World War II was dominated by three approaches: logical positivism, relativism, and Marxism. Literature tended to build on existential philosophy and focus on the subjective experience of the individual. The fine arts, too, often focused on the subjective experience, with painting schools exploring the subconscious and feelings, and in general rejecting traditional values. Architects continued to value functionalism. Musicians continued the attack on tradition by moving increasingly to atonal, dissonant, and experimental music. There has also been a growth of popular culture, with an explosion in cinema, television, radio, and cheap newspapers and novels. However, these products of popular

culture have also influenced elite fine art. Great filmmakers and jazz musicians continue trends established by fine artists.

STUDY QUESTIONS

1. Describe the changing patterns of work and living in a postindustrial society. What jobs are increasing? What is needed to have access to these jobs?

2. Describe how families have changed since World War II. Along with this change has come a change in women's roles, education, and the state's involvement in social programs. Discuss how changing families has influenced these other significant twentieth-century changes.

3. What steps have established churches and individual thinkers made to make religion relevant in the twentieth century? Which do you think have been most successful in keeping people attached to traditional Christian churches?

4. What are some of the discoveries in the physical and biological sciences? Which do you think have made the most impact on our lives?

5. What new approaches have been used extensively in the social sciences to make new advances in knowledge? Which do you think is the most important?

6. What are the main elements of Keynesian economics? Do you see this philosophy implemented in the social and cultural patterns of the twentieth century?

7. Contrast the three trends that dominated philosophical thought after World War II. What kinds of questions do you think each approach might best answer?

8. Twentieth-century literature tended to focus on a more subjective point of view to look at the feelings of individuals. Discuss two twentieth-century authors to demonstrate the truth of this statement.

9. Twentieth-century visual artists also expressed a turning inward for inspiration and a focus on the subjective. Discuss the major styles of painting and the major artists to demonstrate the truth of this statement.

IDENTIFICATION

TRY TO USE EACH OF THESE TERMS AT LEAST ONCE IN ANSWERING THE STUDY QUESTIONS

postindustrial	Second Vatican	John XXIII
John Paul I	Council	Paul Tillich
Harvey Cox	Karl Barth	Max Planck
DNA	relativism	J.M. Keynes
logical positivism	existentialism	L. Wittgenstein
Jean-Paul Sartre	Marxism	James Joyce
Virginia Woolf	T.S. Eliot	Franz Kafka
Thomas Mann	Marcel Proust	Samuel Beckett
Albert Camus	Boris Pasternak	Pablo Picasso
cubism	surrealism	expressionism
functionalism	Frank Lloyd Wright	Arnold Schoenberg

SAMPLE QUESTIONS

1.   What occupations are featured in "postindustrial" societies? (p. 720)

2.   What is the mechanism by which most people enter the middle class? (p. 721)

3.   Since the 1950s in Europe, what group of people has tended to hold the lowest paying and least desirable jobs? (p. 721)

4.   Give some examples of institutions that have grown up to take over functions that families used to perform exclusively. (p. 722)

5.   What were the goals of the women's liberation movement? (p. 723)

6.   What is a "welfare state"? (p. 724)

7.   What did the Second Vatican Council do? (p. 725)

8.   What thinkers attempted to make Christian terms into symbols of personal and social ethics and social revolution? (p. 725)

9.   What is the quantum theory? (p. 727)

10.   What "miracle drugs" greatly reduced disease during the late 1920s and 1930s? (p. 727)

11.   What is the main drawback to the application of medical advances? (p. 727)

12.   What kinds of concepts do logical positivism and analytical philosophy reject? (p. 729)

13.   Who argued that individuals are responsible for their own actions and that they must make up their own rules for their lives? (p. 729)

14.   What authors developed the "stream-of-consciousness" technique that offered new insights into the psyche? (p. 729)

15.   What school of painting attempted to represent the activities of the subconscious mind? (p. 731)

16.   What school of painting attempted to express emotional reactions rather than represent the natural appearance of objects? (p. 731)

17.   Who was the best known American architect of the functional style, who emphasized that form should conform to the materials used? (p. 732)

REVIEW AND ANTICIPATION

1.   Review Adam Smith's laissez-faire economic principles. How were they modified by Keynes? Do you think modern western societies follow more closely Smith or Keynes?

2.   What do you think will be the greatest problems to confront western society in the future?

Chapter 58
Decolonization and the Non-Western World, 1945-Present

OVERVIEW

After World War II, the European powers lost their colonies. These new nations became a force with problems and concerns that the West would increasingly have to take into account.

1. Japan Between East and West. After the war, Japan was occupied by United States forces. During this occupation, Japan received a democratic constitution and many liberal and land reforms. It received aid from the United States which it used to build its industry so effectively that by the 1960s it had become the third greatest industrial power.

2. The Rise of Communist China. In 1945, a civil war broke out for the control of China. Chiang Kai-shek and the Communist, Mao Tse-tung, fought. Mao had support of the people, and Chiang Kai-shek fled to the island of Formosa (Taiwan). Mao introduced five-year plans to industrialize the agricultural China. Against forces of moderation, Mao called a "cultural revolution," which unleashed turmoil but crushed the moderates. Mao's strict communism was moderated after his death by his successor who allowed some movement toward a market economy and some contact with the West.

3. The Korean War. Korea was liberated from the Japanese in 1945 by Soviet forces in the north and American forces in the south. The two forces each established governments in their territories: a Communist dictatorship in the north and a right-wing dictatorship in the south. Both sides wanted to unify the country again. In 1950, North Korea attacked the South. The United Nations with U.S. leadership went to war against North Korea supported by Red China. The war ended without territorial changes. South Korea became industrialized and prosperous.

4. The Revolt of Southern Asia. With the exception of Hong Kong, all the old colonies in Asia achieved their independence. India forced Britain to grant it independence, but religious differences caused the old colony ultimately to be split into three parts: India, Pakistan, Bangladesh. The colony that had the bloodiest struggle freeing itself was French Indochina (Vietnam, Cambodia, Laos). As the French were forced out, the United States entered the war to try to prevent the Communist liberation forces from winning. After much devastation, the United States was forced to leave. North and South Vietnam were united as an independent country, but unrest and violence continued in the region.

5.   The Embattled Middle East. The Middle East is profoundly important strategically and because of the vast reserves of oil. Unfortunately, it is also an area of turmoil. After World War II, when Jews established the State of Israel, the Islamic world was outraged. That has triggered years of warfare and instability in that region. Furthermore, Palestinian refugees destabilized first Jordan, then more seriously, Lebanon, which has continued to be racked by civil war. Palestinians have spread their struggle outside the Middle East by terrorists acts of the Palestinian Liberation Organization. Iran successfully overthrew the American-backed dictatorship of the shah, and introduced a fundamentalist Islamic government. This has not enhanced the stability of the region. There have been continued wars between Iran and Iraq, Iraq and Kuwait, and the United Nations against Iraq. It appears that instability in the region will continue.

6.   The Emancipation of Africa. After World War II, nationalism spread to African colonies. Gradually, colonies were freed, often after violence. Many problems remained: Tribal loyalties often split countries; white governments were unwilling to share power with black constituencies; agricultural and economic problems caused much misery among the population.

7.   Latin America. As part of the Cold War struggles, the United States has supported right-wing dictatorships (often oppressive) in Latin America. These seemed preferable to increasingly popular Communist regimes that seemed to offer a solution to the dramatic problems of poverty. The region remains plagued by such problems.

MAP EXERCISE

1.   On the map of Asia, locate the following countries: China, Japan, North Korea, South Korea, Taiwan, Vietnam, Laos, Cambodia, Thailand, India, Pakistan, Bangladesh, Afghanistan, Confederation of Independent States (old Soviet Union).

2.   The old colony of India ultimately broke into what three independent countries?

3.   What countries fighting wars of independence in Asia should have been of most interest to China?

MAP 58.1 Asia, 1993

4.   On the map of the Middle East, locate the following countries: Iran, Afghanistan, Iraq, Syria, Lebanon, Israel, Jordan, Egypt, Saudi Arabia, Kuwait, Turkey.

5.   What countries would be most threatened by the State of Israel? What country would have been most threatened by Iraq's invasion of Kuwait? What country would have most to fear from Iran's fundamentalist regime? Of all these countries, which do you think will be the most likely to be unstable?

STUDY QUESTIONS

1.   How did Japan acquire a liberal democratic constitution and a highly successful economy? Contrast the experience of Japan with that of other Eastern nations.

2.   Explain how China came to be Communist. Discuss the progress of the revolution: How was industrialization forwarded? What was the "cultural revolution"? What moderated the hard-line Communist stance?

3.   What was the main issue in the Korean War? What countries supported each side? What was the resolution of the war?

4.   How did India achieve independence? Who were its leaders? What problems faced the newly independent country?

5.   Why did the United States get involved in the war in Vietnam (French Indochina)? What was the result of that war? What role did public opinion play in that war?

6.   Discuss the establishment and preservation of the State of Israel. How did the Islamic nations respond? What brought peace between Israel and Egypt? Are there continuing problems in that area today?

7.   What revolutions and wars have taken place in the oil-rich lands of Iran and Iraq? Is this area now stabilized?

8.   The granting of independence did not bring peace and prosperity to the African colonies. Why not? What problems remained? What problems still remain?

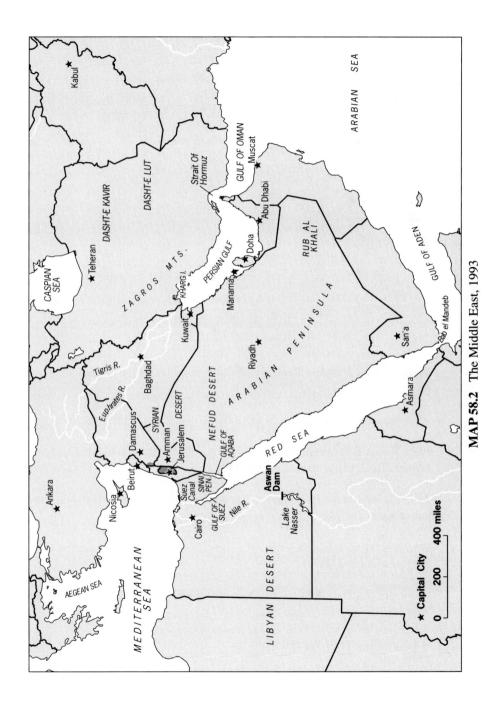

MAP 58.2 The Middle East, 1993

Kabul

ARABIAN SEA

DASHT-E KAVIR

DASHT-E LUT

Strait Of
Hormuz

GULF OF OMAN

Muscat

Abu Dhabi

CASPIAN
SEA

Teheran

ZAGROS MTS.

KHARG I.

PERSIAN GULF

Doha

RUB AL
KHALI

Manama

GULF OF ADEN

Bab el Mandeb

Kuwait

San'a

Tigris R.

Baghdad

Riyadh

ARABIAN PENINSULA

Asmara

Euphrates R.

SYRIAN

Damascus

NEFUD DESERT

DESERT

Amman

Ankara

Beirut

Jerusalem

GULF OF
AQABA

RED SEA

Nicosia

Suez
Canal

SINAI
PEN.

Cairo

GULF OF
SUEZ

Nile R.

Aswan
Dam

MEDITERRANEAN
SEA

AEGEAN SEA

LIBYAN DESERT

Lake
Nasser

★ Capital City

0   200   400 miles

263

IDENTIFICATION

TRY TO USE EACH OF THESE TERMS AT LEAST ONCE IN ANSWERING
THE STUDY QUESTIONS AND MAP EXERCISES

Douglas MacArthur	Chiang Kai-shek	Mao Tse-tung
Great Leap Forward	cultural	M.K. Gandhi
Deng Xiaoping	revolution	J. Nehru
Ho Chi Minh	Balfour	Nasser
Six-Day War	Declaration	Anwar Sadat
PLO	Yasir Arafat	Khomeini
apartheid	F.W. de Klerk	Allende
Sandinistas	Fidel Castro	Batista

SAMPLE QUESTIONS

1.   What form of government was created in Japan after its defeat in the war?
(p. 736)

2.   Where did the Chinese Nationalists end up establishing their government? (p.
738)

3.   When was the People's Republic of China admitted to the United Nations?
(p. 739)

4.   What tactics did Gandhi use to force the British out of India? (p. 740)

5.   What family dominated Indian politics after the death of Gandhi, supplying
the next three prime ministers? (p. 740)

6.   After the independence of India, what was the only remaining British colony
left in Asia? (p. 741)

7.   Who was the Communist leader of Vietnam's movement for liberation from
the French? (p. 741)

8.   When did the United States withdraw its armed forces from Vietnam? (p.
743)

9.   What people were displaced when the State of Israel was formed? (pp. 745-
746)

10.   What kind of government was introduced in Iran after the overthrow of the dictatorship of the shah? (p. 746)

11.   In what two African nations was there struggle after independence between all-white governments and the black majority of the population? (p. 747)

12.   What was the purpose of the Organization of American States? (p. 750)

REVIEW AND ANTICIPATION

1.   Both the French Revolution and the Russian Revolution succumbed to excess violence in an attempt to preserve revolutionary fervor. What was a comparable movement in the Chinese revolution?

2.   Review the ideals that shaped the Cold War and the fears that dominated the United States during that period. How does that help explain the United States' involvement in Vietnam, a war of colonial liberation?

3.   What parts of the non-Western world do you expect to be continuing sources of instability?

Chapter 59
The Collapse of Communism
and New Realities

OVERVIEW

In the 1990s it seems that three developments mark the beginning of a new era: 1) the collapse of communism, 2) integration of Western Europe, and 3) increasing economic strength in the Pacific Rim. These trends will likely shape events in the future.

1. The Collapse of Communism. The collapse of communism marks the end of the Cold War. Communism had been weakened by growing economic problems and expensive military actions and the arms race. To try to restore the ailing economy, Gorbachev instituted reforms that increased freedom. This loosening of the repressive Soviet society allowed revolutions to take place in all the Communist countries of Eastern Europe, in which the Stalinist governments were replaced with democratic regimes. Finally, the Soviet Union itself collapsed as a political union and was replaced by a loose confederation of states and many completely independent ones.

2. Integration, the Rise of Germany, and Conservatism in Europe. During the late 1980s and 1990s, Europe has built on the Common Market and has moved toward greater integration of its economies and politics. This movement toward unity has the potential to create a prosperous and powerful block. Further integration has taken place with the reunification of Germany, which places Germany in a strong position in the new Europe. Politically, as communism has collapsed, Europe has moved to the right to become more conservative.

3. The United States: Military Ascendancy and Economic Problems. After the fall of communism, the United States remained the world's only military superpower. Yet, the cost was high, and in the 1990s the United States suffers from a huge national debt that has seriously weakened the economy. It is unclear how this combination of military strength and economic trouble will be resolved.

4. The Pacific Rim, Japan, and China. Areas in the Pacific Rim that offer political stability and a good labor force have attracted investment. Consequently they are becoming more prosperous and competitive in the international market. Japan became a world economic power in the 1980s. China has great economic potential, and the Communist government has encouraged economic enterprise without corresponding political reform. This led to demonstrations for democracy in 1989 which were severely repressed.

In general, East Asia will challenge the economic dominance that the West has enjoyed for centuries.

5.   <u>Problems of the Present and Future.</u> In spite of many positive developments for increased peace and prosperity in the West, many problems remain. Ethnic conflict threatens peace, and the Middle East continues to be a source of tension. Economic growth cannot be taken for granted, and environmental problems have continued to grow. The relatively rich West can no longer ignore the problems of the less affluent world. These problems will require all the continued energy of the West.

MAP EXERCISE

See map on p. 268.

1.   On the map of Eastern Europe, write in all the names of the countries that are outlined.

2.   Number all the countries that had revolutions to free themselves from Communist governments in the order in which they achieved freedom.

STUDY QUESTIONS

1.   What caused the fall of communism in the Soviet Union? What were the long-term and immediate causes? How was the fall brought about?

2.   How did the Communist governments of Eastern Europe fall?

3.   What steps are being taken to increase the integration of Europe? Why will these make Europe an even more significant force than it had been in the past?

4.   What are the strengths and weaknesses of the United States after the fall of its opponent in the Cold War?

5.   Why have the countries of the Pacific Rim and Japan enjoyed such an economic boom? Is this likely to continue?

6.   Contrast Gorbachev's retreat from communism with changes that have taken place in China. In what aspects have the Chinese increased the freedoms in their society? In what ways have they not?

7.   Describe the environmental problems that will continue to trouble us for some time to come.

MAP 59.1 Upheaval in Eastern Europe since 1989

IDENTIFICATION

TRY TO USE EACH OF THESE TERMS AT LEAST ONCE IN ANSWERING THE STUDY QUESTIONS AND MAP EXERCISES

glasnost   *perestroika*   M. Gorbachev
B. Yeltsin   Solidarity   E. Honecker
Maastricht   Common Market   H. Kohl
  Treaty

SAMPLE QUESTIONS

1.   What factors reduced the productivity of Communist workers? (p. 754)

2.   To what does *perestroika* refer? (p. 755)

3.   To what does *glasnost* refer? (p. 755)

4.   What Eastern European state quickly fell into ethnic and religious civil war after it was freed from Soviet control? (p. 758)

5.   What problems remained in the states of the old Soviet Union after the fall of communism? (p. 759)

6.   By 1992, how many members were there in the European Community? (p. 760)

7.   What was the Maastricht Treaty to achieve? (p. 760)

8.   When was Germany reunified? (p. 761)

9.   What is the United States' main economic problem in the 1990s? (p. 761)

10.   In what industries did Japan become a world leader in the 1980s? (p. 762)

11.   What areas along the Pacific Rim have become economically prosperous? (p. 762)

REVIEW AND ANTICIPATION

1.   Review the nationalist movements in the Balkans and the area of the old Austro-Hungarian Empire, and recall the instability that was expressed there

especially before World War I. Does the ethnic violence in Yugoslavia continue this tradition?

2.   Of the problems described in the text as confronting the West in the future, which do you think will be most pressing?